"*Don't Look Back* brings good news for weary, sad, and cynical Methodists: You are loved and chosen. There is a place and future for you in the relentless renewing work of God in our world. His insights are tough and encouraging, practical, clear-eyed, honest, relational, humble in service, Christ-centered, and so hopeful! This book invites us to dig deeper into our faith and ultimate mission beyond denominational mechanics and brokenness—bearing witness to what God is doing. This is a word not only for Methodists but for anyone who shares a radical Christian commitment and calling."

—Joni Sancken, professor of homiletics, United Theological Seminary, Dayton, OH

"In *Don't Look Back* Will Willimon is an 'equal opportunity' truth-teller. No one and nothing is off limits, including himself and especially not the institutional church. He encourages healthy grieving for what is no more but eschews syrupy nostalgia. He preaches, teaches, meddles, prods, and probes, all in the hope that we will fasten our attention on the resurrected Jesus and join him where he is at work."

—Gregory V. Palmer, resident bishop, Ohio West area, The United Methodist Church

"In equal parts funny, frank, and provocative, Willimon's impassioned plea for 'togetherness' is worth serious reflection for all tempted to separate from The United Methodist Church. Staring soberly at American Methodism's losses, *Don't Look Back* is filled with unyielding hope for a church willing to let go of the past, redefine its purpose, and get on mission with the resurrected, living Christ."

—Roger Ross, former director of congregational excellence, Missouri Conference; coach with Spiritual Leadership, Inc

"Please take this book's invitation from Will Willimon to get into the conversation about the future. The world is not going to snap back to any pre-pandemic, pre-populist political form in the near future. So, to talk about a real future Will gives us the good things to remember from the past, a dose of reality about the present, and good questions about the future. This book is a gift to get us talking about a future church that reflects Christ's purpose, not our preferences."

—Gil Rendle, consultant; former senior vice president, The Texas Methodist Foundation; widely recognized as one of Methodism's wisest guides

"Several hurrahs for Willimon: For his great use of scripture; for effectively pushing readers on specific points and into seeing the larger issues at hand; for clear framing of hard questions and forcing attention to them; for pointed dismissal of easy answers to what he shows are deeply rooted, institution-wide specters haunting leadership at all levels; but especially and as usual in Willimon's books, readability."

—Russell E. Richey, dean emeritus, Candler School of Theology, and William R. Cannon Distinguished Professor of Church History Emeritus

"This book blends history, theology, personal narrative, and biblical scholarship to offer concrete ways to move forward to a reformed church of which John Wesley would be proud."

—Andy Langford, senior pastor, Central United Methodist Church, Concord, NC; scholar and expert on worship, evangelism, and preaching; editor of *The United Methodist Book of Worship*

"Willimon does not disappoint. He writes what so many are reluctant to say about schism over one issue promoted with language from secular culture wars but missing the words of Jesus and John Wesley. He also incisively captures the sadness of the loss that may occur for no good reason."

—Lovett H. Weems, Jr., Distinguished Professor of Church Leadership Emeritus, Wesley Theological Seminary, Washington, DC

"Willimon shows us how to honor and grieve the past while also growing into a new and vital way of being Jesus's church. He teaches us how to look for what God is up to in our specific setting and to have the courage to be a part of God's mission. Even if he is writing for his own Methodist friends, he is speaking powerfully to this Episcopal Bishop."

—Jake Owensby, Bishop of the Episcopal Church in Western Louisiana; author of *Looking for God in Messy Places*

"*Don't Look Back* is replete with infectious optimism and hope that God will ensure the accomplishment of the *missio Dei*. Willimon offers guidance to local churches seeking to reinvent their missional focus, embracing moral imagination and prophetic vision in reaching the unchurched."

—Donald E. Williams, pastor, Remington UMC, Fauquier County, VA

"Willimon is telling the story about *your* congregation, *your* community, and *our* faith and witness. He is an unrepentant enthusiast for the Gospel who relies on its promises and audaciously writes less about dispiriting decline and more about tenacious perseverance. The book is packed with local wisdom and hands-on ideas. As we race to keep up, we find we are too impatient to get on with making a faithful difference to allow much time for brooding about denominational preoccupations and disputes. *Don't Look Back* shows us a path forward that's full of thanksgiving and hope."

—Neil Alexander, president and publisher emeritus, The United Methodist Publishing House

Will Willimon

DON'T
LOOK
BACK

Methodist Hope for
What Comes Next

Abingdon Press
Nashville

DON'T LOOK BACK:
Methodist Hope for What Comes Next

Copyright © 2022 by William H. Willimon

Library of Congress Control Number: 2022943213

ISBN: 978-1-7910-2789-6

Scripture quotations unless noted otherwise are from the Common English Bible. Copyright © 2011 by the Common English Bible. All rights reserved. Used by permission. www.CommonEnglishBible.com.

"Call to Disaffiliate from the United Methodist Church," March 2022, Fred B. Suggs, used with permission.

Citations from the "Transitional Book of Doctrines and Discipline of the Global Methodist Church" are from https://globalmethodist.org/what-we-believe/.

The Book of Discipline of the United Methodist Church (Nashville: The United Methodist Publishing House, 2019).

The United Methodist Hymnal (Nashville: The United Methodist Publishing House, 1989).

MANUFACTURED IN THE UNITED STATES OF AMERICA

*In memory of Bessie B. Parker, first ordained woman
in the South Carolina Conference of The United Methodist Church
and in hope that what God accomplished through Bessie's ministry
God continues.*

CONTENTS

INTRODUCTION

Jesus said to him, "No one who puts a hand on the plow and looks back is fit for God's kingdom."

—Luke 9:62

I've written on United Methodist renewal, reorganization, and rejuvenation. Seminarians, new member classes in congregations, and pastors have made me a partner in their ministries. I'm grateful. My previous Methodist books hoped to improve our church. Now's the time to be more bold.

After some stormy years, for the first time in a while, Methodists are separating. We're also coming out of a pandemic that has accelerated our crises and intensified our pain (graying and aging of clergy and laity, decline in membership and worship attendance, financial stress, political polarities, and widening racial disparities) that began long before the pandemic.

I say, let's have a decent burial for yesterday's good intentions and then partner with the Holy Spirit in creating tomorrow's church.

When Jesus cast his disciples into the world, he told them to travel light (Luke 10:4). That's why some pastors and congregations have made these opportune years of Holy Spirit–induced innovation, creation of new ministries, courageous pruning of old programs, and rediscovery/reassertion of core Wesleyan convictions and mission.

Are we at Good Friday ending or Easter beginning? Maybe a bit of both. I hope to help Methodist pastors and congregations —as well as our chaplains, camp directors, and those who minister in our hundreds of homes for children or the aging—to answer, *What next for the churches called Methodist?*

I began research on this book the week a committee (!) decided to delay General Conference. Who cares? None of your necessary work requires anything to be done or not be done at the general church level. The Holy Spirit is God going local. I'll say little about the demise of old denominations or the birth pangs of new ones. No fundamental problem of a Methodist congregation can be solved either by leaving or preserving the UMC. The most surprising Holy Spirit provocations are not in denominations, old or new, but in Methodist congregations who jump on board with God's mission to God's world, one neighborhood at a time.

God begins locally in order to save universally. Read the Bible. The future belongs to pastors and congregations who refuse to be distracted by denominational conflict or to use a pandemic as an excuse for inaction. God's future is for those who ask tough questions, come up with surprising answers, and dare better to align themselves with their core identity and purpose as the Body of Christ in motion. Your congregation, for any of its faults, is Christ's big idea to put right what's wrong with the world.

Here's a book about problems that no book can solve. That's why my research consisted not of reading books but of interviewing hundreds of Methodists, asking them, *Wherein is our hope? What's next? Got any clues about what God's up to? How can your congregation hitch on? What should we stop doing so we can begin what God now calls us to do? What are appropriate goals and mission strategies, and what sort of pastoral leadership is required as we attempt to keep up with Christ (peripatetic Savior) as he moves us into a future that's his? From the first, Christians never asked, "Has God got a future?" The question was, "Will we be part of God's future or not?"*

You and your congregation are God's answer to all these questions, God's hope.

Though I urge you not to waste time looking back, I hope you remember the story of how John Wesley reconstituted the church by inventing a yearly gathering of his traveling lay preachers, the Annual Conference. Wesley opened the meeting asking, *What to teach? How to teach? What to do?* This book is a contemporary response to Wesley's historic questions.

But Father John never limited his holy conferencing to consideration of merely human strategies, plans, and proposals. Shortly after answering the three questions, the Annual Conference moved forward by asking about God: *What may we reasonably believe to be God's design, in raising up the Preachers called Methodists? What's God up to in birthing and in blessing the rise of Methodist Christians?* Ah, that's the question.

Methodists were God's idea before John Wesley's; the church is the only institution that can neither birth nor sustain itself. So the Holy Spirit will not let us be paralyzed by looking in the rearview mirror, nor leave us alone to devise a few workable, humanly fabricated tactics for institutional self-preservation. The love of Christ incites us to dare a theological construal of our present moment. As always, it's a redemptive God's self-assignment to get us out of any mess we're in. So here's our great hope: God refuses to leave the future of The United Methodist Church solely up to us.

Funny, how a redeeming God uses crises, conflict, sadness, and disruption to bring hopeful life out of what we thought was naught but loss and death. Though Wesleyans have always been against gambling, this book bets that God has given us the resources in our originating Wesleyan vision to guide us if we bodaciously take up Christ's gambit, *Come on, I dare you. Don't look back. Walk alongside me as I utilize you in my mission to reclaim the world that belongs to me.*

Will Willimon
The Twenty-Fourth of May, 2022
The two-hundred eighty-fourth anniversary of John
Wesley's "heart strangely warmed" at Aldersgate, London

Visit
abingdonpress.com/dontlookback
to find free resources for pastors and congregations,
including a Leadership Resource Guide and a Video Series.
(See page 172 for additional information.)

Because the most important work we Methodists must do can't be done on our own, let us open with prayer:

Lord Jesus, we give thanks that, whatever you're up to, you have chosen to do it not without us. Calling flawed, finite, fickle failures like us was your big idea for how to save your world. Before we knew how to call upon you, you called on us and assigned us work in your encroaching reign. Give us faith that you knew what you were doing when you summoned the likes of us Methodists to be your church.

To be honest, sometimes we get discouraged. Do our promised prayers, presence, gifts, service, and witness make much difference? After the pandemic, what? Will empty pews and flagging budgets defeat us? Will threatened schisms and separations, the world's cultural shifts, scorn, or indifference kill us? We don't know.

But it's a comfort to know that you know. Keep working on us so that we might continue working for you. Give us the future we can't give ourselves. Make us believe that when you raised up a movement called Methodist, you were on to something grand.

In the present hour, embolden us to risk the pain that comes with change. Give us room to mourn, but don't let grief get the best of us. Remind us of Wesleyan history, but let not our love of the past keep us from being part of your future. Breathe your Holy Spirit upon us that we may receive new birth, second wind, detoxification, and reinvention as present foretaste of promised resurrection.

Give us the courage to speak truth to one another, and to listen, particularly when what we hear is painful, expectant of the possibility that you are using the testimony of someone we don't like to teach us truth we wouldn't know without their testimony.

Of all those you could have called to be your bodily presence in your world, you made us Methodists. Thanks for including us (in order to commission us), for assigning work (that's impossible to accomplish alone), for giving us more future with you than past (refusing to let our death, sin, stupidity, timidity, and spinelessness have the last word on Wesleyanism).

Amen.

Chapter 1

BY GOD'S GRACE, HOPE

Methodism as we have known it is ending, dying from a dozen wounds, some self-inflicted, some wreaked by a world that's God's but hasn't gotten the news. Methodism as we have yet to experience it is being born. The new Methodism could be better than the old, for all we know. Just what you would expect from a God who, from the first, loves to raise the dead and make a way when we thought we were at a dead end.

Kicked by social forces and sicknesses we neither caused nor control, we've been pushed into a church that's different from the one we joined. God has called us to be the church during a divisive time in the United States. Infected by political divisions (mostly among white voters), racial antipathy (say, "I've never seen America more divided," and it's a sure sign you are white), suspicion and distrust of leaders ("Bishops are buffoons"), and tensions between the generations ("Why won't the kids come to church?"). Our self-signifiers "traditional" and "progressive" are more determinative of the fights we pick on social media than the label "Methodist Christian." Other denominations ask, "Weren't you Methodists always ecumenical? You're in fellowship with Catholics who are wrong on the ordination of women and clergy celibacy, yet you can't keep conversing with Methodists about marriage? What gives?"

It's my contention that our divisions and separations are less menacing than the specter of our expiring. An organization with a median age of sixty-three is a group in accelerated devolution. Farewell to the church many of us loved, the church that introduced us to Christ and made us disciples. UMC, you'll be in our thoughts and prayers.

Still, in any grieving, the trick is to grieve like Christians. As Paul put it to one of his morose congregations, we don't "mourn like others who don't have any hope" (1 Thess 4:13). We grieve, yes, but our greatest grief is framed by God-given hope. The most searing Psalms of Lament deny grief the last word. (Psalms 51 and 130 come to mind.) Christians don't have to put on a smiley face and deny our loss; we have hope that's "a safe and secure anchor for our whole being" (Heb 6:19), hope that won't let death and dying have the final say.

My minor book on major Methodist beliefs *(This We Believe: The Core of Wesleyan Faith and Practice)* ended, as orthodox Christian theology usually does, with hope. When it's all said and done, a resurrected Christ enables us to hope that it's not over until God says it's over. *Don't Look Back* begins with forward-looking hope, because if specifically Christian hope isn't true, there's no use having this conversation.

Hope in a Savior Who Defeats Our Hopelessness

Hopelessness was me when I was deposited by the bishop at a forlorn inner-city Methodist church in the early 1980s.

The congregation had been formed in the 1960s when the pastor of my home church asked twelve families to leave our congregation and plant a new church on the north side of town. (Ah, the good old days when large Methodist congregations felt a missionary obligation to birth new churches.) A forward-looking, suburban congregation built a proudly modern building and enjoyed spectacular growth. But after initial growth (1,000 members by the end of its first decade), decline began (as old-timers recalled congregational history) when their hot shot preacher shook the saints with his sermons condemning the Viet Nam war. The prophet was succeeded by a deflated pastor, sent to the church four years after he should have retired. Further losses. The young families who began the church aged out. Few of their children stayed past high school. By the time I got there, the congregation had shrunk to less than three hundred (no matter what the Conference Journal alleged) with a median age of sixty.

Grass growing in the parking lot, seven (count 'em, seven) empty Sunday school rooms, aging HVAC, leaking roof, and broken budget infected the remaining faithful few with hopelessness.

"Son, give this congregation one honest-to-God victory or you're good as dead," advised an older pastor.

"That appointment will shut him up," the District Superintendent was reputed to have smirked. "He won't talk his way out of this."

This is not only the sort of church that can be dumped upon a pastor in mainline, oldline, sidelined, itinerant Protestantism but also what one gets when serving a Savior who is a sucker for—and a redeemer of—lost causes. A dying church is just one more opportunity for Mr. Resurrection and the Life to do his thing (John 11:25).

So Patsy and I threw ourselves into revitalization of the congregation, without measurable response. In my first miserable year, decline continued unabated, demonstrating that my perky preaching, breathless pastoral care, adroit administration, even my suffering with the youth on a five-day camping trip (lying on an iron bunk praying to God for dawn to come), couldn't give this ailing congregation a future.

Amid my self-doubts and the congregation's defeatism, I was forced to go deeper spiritually. A little prayer at the beginning of the day, an hour of biblical study to prepare a sermon didn't lift the luggage to lead a church whose prognosis was grim. In short, the work that needed doing was impossible without God.

I was empty-handed, forced to ask for outside help. An experienced (though inexpensive) coach was found. "How is your tolerance for pain? Pray that God will give you the guts to face the truth, then the grace to find a way to share it without their killing you. Still, they are so far down they've not the oomph to resist you."

"These people have forgotten how to be Methodists," the consultant told me after a day of interviews with our leaders. "They like not being Baptist. They think their moderate, middle-of-the-road Methodist-believing is a gift from God. But their muddled sense of mission is too modest to save this church. Don't get them on a plane to do mission in Zimbabwe; get them in gear doing good in this neighborhood. You believe in them half as much as the Lord does?" asked the consultant, his eyes drilling into my soul.

After just over a year, I figured I had earned enough congregational trust to tell the truth. On a Wednesday night the board met in the dingy little chapel where the congregation was born. I showed them the numbers—giving patterns, average age of the membership, worship attendance, children, and baptisms. "According to my calculations, the last Methodist will turn out the lights fifteen years from now."

There were tears. Some anger.

"Why weren't we told?"

"The bishop has never sent us good preachers." Ouch.

"If you would preach less intellectual sermons, we'd have better attendance." That hurt.

"The Methodist church has gone full-on liberal and now we're paying for it." Give me a break.

"It's just as well that the malcontents and naysayers left," one old-timer wheezed, defensively.

After the naming and blaming, someone said, "I want there to be a church here for my grandchildren, but I wouldn't know where to begin to make that happen."

I laid aside my charts and graphs and said, "The good news is, I think we can grow, which is the only way we can survive. I also believe I know how. The bad news? It won't be painless. We must decide to grow, or else we will become just another Methodist church on the way out."

Someone finally said, "Tell us what we'd need to do to have a tomorrow."

Back to the depressing graphs. "See this line here? Note that it drifts downward sometime around 1975."

"That's when Preacher Smith was here," someone called out. "His left-wing sermons drove away some of our best-paying members."

"No, I think the problem wasn't your pastors' sermons, it was that your pastors (including your present pastor), and the church as a whole, lost the adventurous spirit that got us here in the first place. We stopped being a church for this neighborhood, and made the fatal mistake of becoming a church for the sake of church. We lost our monopoly but acted as if ours was the only way to worship God in this part of town.

"For our first decade, we had growth. Nearly all of our members came from this neighborhood. But then, in the early seventies, we ceased attracting new members. We stopped thinking about everyone else's children and focused on our own. The number of baptisms declined. But attendance and giving gave us the illusion that we were okay. By the end of the seventies, the young families who founded this church had moved to other neighborhoods and commuted back for Sunday services. Our average age began to rise, and the number of children declined dramatically."

"But why?" asked a plaintive voice.

"The simple answer? We lost our neighborhood. Or, should I say, our neighborhood lost us? We became a church of commuters who loved one another, who found God here in our worship and life together, but who were inwardly focused."

I couldn't help myself; I began to preach: "The first Bible verse I memorized as a kid was John 3:16. 'For God so loved me and people who look a lot like me and with whom I'm the most comfortable that God gave....' No! Jesus didn't die just for the church. Christ wants it all! Looking at our numbers, it appears that Jesus is unkind to a church that forgets how to join him in his retaking of his world. We've made church inward; Jesus Christ won't let us be anything but outward."

Then one of our founding members asked the decisive, frightening question: "Will, do you think there's any hope?"

That was my cue. I rattled off quickly the four or five things we were doing right: new signage on nearby streets and in our building, improved music program, exterior lighting, trained hosts at our doors on Sunday, a better-looking brochure.

"But we've got to do more," I said. "I'm not sure which specific steps we need to take, but I promise, after tonight, I'll start moving in the direction of reclamation of our neighborhood. Tonight I claim four blocks in every direction of our church as our turf. Where God has planted us. Our responsibility. Our pulpit. I promise to spend less time caring for our members and more time finding out which of our neighbors needs what we've got to offer. You'll have to support me and interpret my move from being just a pastor to a coordinator of missionaries. I don't exactly know which steps to take, but after tonight, I know where we're moving. Let's go!"

The meeting ended with a benediction from one of our founding members. "Let's all try real hard to believe that the Lord was on to something when he began this church in Bentley and Eva Lou's living room twenty-six years ago. Amen."

We scuttled all church officers and committees (along with their monthly meetings) and slimmed down governance to an eight-person task force. I recommended the membership of the task force: those who knew how to start things, who didn't mind taking risks, and who could move with urgency.

Growth in membership became our priority. None of our problems—financial, morale, building maintenance, dearth of youth and children—could be solved without fixing our shrinking membership. Every dime we spent, every hour I worked, the test for any new initiative—*growth.*

We junked plans to refurbish the church parlor and, instead, renovated the nursery and children's rooms. I promised the church I'd share the ways that I had changed my daily schedule in order to lead with their priorities.

We paid only half of our Conference apportionments. "We're now spending a greater portion of our income on mission than the Conference. If our efforts pay off, the Conference can count on more cash; if we fail, well…"

I went on a crash church-growth reading course. I preached a sermon series called "Mission Possible," in which I presented the gospel as God's mission. Each sermon was heavy on examples of individuals and churches who got geared up for mission and evangelism. At the end of each sermon I said, "Okay. You've watched Jesus in action in mission. Now I want everyone, yes you, to take one of those cards in the pew rack and complete this sentence: *Because Jesus's mission was to _____, therefore our congregation's mission should be to _____.* Drop your cards in the box at the back as you leave."

With many flops and false starts but a few successes and victories, God got mixed up among us in new, life-giving ways. These were some of our most memorable wins (which I celebrated as if they were the *eschaton*):

- We selected a set of stereotypical grandparents and commissioned them to visit every baby born on our turf. By checking the newborn list at the local hospital, it was easy to find where new babies lived. About a week after the baby was brought home, our official "Baby Visitors" showed up on the doorstep saying, "Can we see our new neighbor?"

The generic grandparents bore a children's Bible storybook ("Never too soon to start reading to the baby," the parents were told), a pamphlet on baby care, and a set of disposable diapers. "Our church is right down the street. Children are our top priority. When you visit, you'll find a group of talented, vetted caregivers to greet you. We also have a new Parents Morning Out program. First two visits free. Childrens' bulletins for worship too. Just want you to know that you don't have to be parents alone. We're here to help."

For the first time in a decade, growth.

- We awoke to the presence of an elementary school across the street from the church. I took the principal to lunch so I could ask, "Could your after-school tutoring program use five or six vetted, able, retired school teachers?"

   Those after-school tutors were coached to eventually find the right time to tell their students, "I'd like to meet your parents." Nearly all were invited into their homes where they invited the parents to church. We received the first visitors who were not of our ethnicity.

- When one of our older members was fired from his executive job and went into depression on his couch, the Holy Spirit prodded me to ask, "Weren't you head of personnel? I bet you have skills that some of our young adults badly need." I got him together with three twenty-somethings who were having difficulty finding their way into the workforce.

   "The man's a genius," gushed one. "I was a business major, and nobody cared enough to teach me what to say to get a job."

   The Holy Spirit, working through a pushy pastor, prodded our Job Coach to say to the three, "Love working with you guys but if we're to continue, each of you must find a friend to join us, somebody who's not a member of a church." The town's hottest young adult ministry was born.

"There's just about no problem we face in this church that can't be solved by more Methodists," was our mantra. The more we noticed our neighbors, the more we discovered the unique ministries of our members, the more we grew. Fifty new members joined during the first year of our mission emphasis.

"Turns out, lots of folks around here want to do something to make this town better; they just hadn't found a church that would show them how," mused one of our leaders.

In a year, we had more hope than we could handle. When I missed the August meeting of the Finance Committee, they baffled me by voting a 10% increase in the new budget.

"You must be joking," I told the chair. "This church has always had a record of bad finances. That big a jump is nuts," I pronounced.

Two weeks into our Fall Stewardship Emphasis the chair used that Sunday's "Stewardship Minute" to say, "I never dared even to hope that I'd be making this announcement. You have, as of this week, pledged next year's budget in full."

Spontaneous applause.

"Ten percent increase over last year!" Again, applause.

"Now as I recall, someone said, when the Finance Committee launched out on faith, 'You will never pledge that budget.' Someone who even said, 'That's nuts.' Now, who had so little faith?"

Gales of anti-clerical laughter.

"Turns out," he continued, "we believed his 'money follows mission' sermon more than he did." Haw, haw, haw.

"That's enough, George. Sit down," said I, in love.

Laughter, applause, general rejoicing at the irony of a deficit of hope in the guy who's supposed to be leading hope. Tell me there's not a Holy Spirit.

I could go on. My guestimate is that for every one of these mission initiatives that worked, three bombed. (How were we to know that no neighbors needed a community garden, dog obedience classes, Saturday Night at the Movies, study of Major Methodist Beliefs, or a food pantry?) Yet during those four years I got to experience the fun of a congregation stepping up to their baptismal promises and playing a part in God so loving the world.

I wish I could say that the congregation continued to grow and to connect. A succession of pastors—none apparently appointed to lead the mission of a church that was determined to live—came and went. Valiant, committed laity alone can't sustain a congregation's mission. Those laity who had a missional view of the church, who were demanding and visionary, drifted into more vital congregations. The few who stayed looked back, reverting to what was most comfortable: internal caregiving. "We are a loving, caring congregation," they reassure one another as they pass away peacefully.

Last year the church that got unstuck in the early eighties became a part-time pastoral appointment, testimonial to the difficulty of keeping up with the mission of Jesus Christ, to the lethal effects of inwardness, and to the poor administration of the United Methodist appointive system. It's vital for a congregation to focus on mission, but when bishops don't honor a congregation's mission in clergy appointments, it's deadly.

I look back to one of my early appointments to make this point: *I didn't do that.* Few of the good ideas for mission in our neighborhood, none of my restlessness in the face of decline and death, little of the growth came from me, nor even from a group of determined laity or a savvy consultant. Hopefulness arose—as Christian hope always does—as a gracious gift of a God determined to have a family. To God be the glory.

And yet, to give ourselves credit, we did try to face the truth. We asked for help. We prayed and sought the advice of those who were already following Christ into the world he loves. We had no expectation of help from the General or Annual Conference. Little time was wasted looking back either in nostalgia or assigning blame. Daring to hope that God still had a purpose for the likes of us, we risked following Jesus, even when we weren't sure where he was going.

I'm grateful I got a front row seat on the Holy Spirit's machinations, setting in motion the Body of Christ. What a privilege to participate in the work of a God who chooses to save the world, one neighborhood at a time, through Methodists.

Paul wrote to one of his beleaguered congregations, "We even take pride in our problems, because we know that trouble produces endurance, endurance produces character, and character produces hope" (Rom 5:3-4). Of this, I am a witness. When someone says to me, "That church is dead, died two pastors ago," or "No way that congregation will turn around," I think back to a church that rediscovered its God-given mission. While I don't know that we took "pride in our problems," we at least endured facing up to them. The fruit of it all, as Paul promised the Romans, was hope.

By the way, four decades later I tried to apply what I had learned at that early appointment to a declining inner-city, part-time appointment the bishop gave me on the verge of retirement. Though I entered into it with enthusiasm, lots of experience, prayer, and determination, I failed. Decline was unabated by truth-telling, endurance, and earnestness. True, I was only there a year, but I recall my disappointment in order to remind you that being Christ's church is risky, prone-to-failure work. Read the statistics on UMC attendance and giving patterns, and it will take a miracle for you to have hope for a vital Methodist future.

Good news. A miracle is just what we have in Jesus Christ. For a resurrecting God, divine work that gives hope to the hopeless is just another day at the office.

If God's got no use for Methodism, then there's no hope. But if your congregation can find a way to hitch on to what God's already up to in your part of the world, then from what I've seen, there'll be more hope than you can handle.

Biblical Hope for Methodists

My experience with a congregation that moved from hopelessness to hopefulness is empirical verification of biblical hope. "Hope" appears in scripture, Old Testament and New, as both a noun and a verb, as something hoped for, as a human attitude, and as a disposition toward the future.

To the Romans, Paul speaks of "the hope of God's glory." Although we don't know the sources of First Church Rome's fear and consternation, I'd wager that they had greater justification for their flagging hope than we. Having extolled the grace Christ has given us, Paul says, "We have access by faith into this grace in which we stand through him, and we boast in the hope of God's glory" (Rom 5:2). Hanging on by their fingernails, beset by imperial enemies as well as internal divisions, this fragile gathering of the first Christians is told to "boast in the hope of God's glory"?

Please note that the Romans' boasting is in God's glory and not in their astute analysis or their glorious powers of organizational rehabilitation. Old Testament and New, whenever *hope* is used as noun (Greek: *elpis*) or verb (*elpizein*), hope is always dependent upon God's fidelity and goodness. More than wishful thinking, biblical hope is a reasonable, confident expectation that's based upon the nature and work of God—past, present, and future.

Hanging in there, anticipating good from bad, are aspects of biblical hope:

> Israel, wait for the LORD!
>> Because faithful love is with the LORD;
>> because great redemption is with our God!
>>> (Ps 130:7)

The hopes that Jesus's followers had for the redemption of Israel were dashed by his death. To their surprise, God made a way when they thought there was no way and gave hope for a future they couldn't give themselves. "If all we have to hope in is ourselves and our efforts," said Paul, "we have no hope" (1 Cor 15:19, paraphrased).

When things seem hopeless, we hang in there out of faith that God shall at last, after all is said and done by us, have the last word. Thus, Paul tells squabbling First Church Corinth to "stand firm, unshakable, excelling in the work of the Lord as always, because you know that your labor isn't going to be for nothing in the Lord" (1 Cor 15:58). If we keep trying to be the Body of Christ in motion, keep struggling to stay together, hope makes us do it.

Everywhere "hope" appears in the Bible, it's always connected to and solely dependent upon a good and loving God.

(Implication: If God is not who Methodists say God is—Jesus Christ, raised from the dead, reconciling the world to himself—there's no hope.)

The beloved "Serenity Prayer" of AA—with its petition for the courage to change what we can, acceptance of what can't change, and wisdom to know the difference—applies to the church. We can humbly ask for the grace to learn to live with what we can't impact (General Conference, errant Bishops, the Institute on Religion and Democracy) and to change what we can (your local church).

However, note anything missing from the Serenity Prayer? *God.* We are not the only actors. In this book I'm going to talk about best practices and proven methods to give your church a future. But human work alone cannot do this.

We have hope amid our present struggles, not because we've got certainty about the future, but because we are clear about who God is and what God is up to. We don't know what the future holds, but we know Who holds the future. Our hope is not wishful thinking; it's reasonable Methodist expectation based upon all that we know of God—Jesus Christ.

A God Who Defeats Our Hopelessness

Cynicism (the belief that our noble goals are mostly motivated by self-interest and that criticism is more intelligent than courage) is less demanding than hope. Rather than risk engagement, setting goals and strategizing to achieve them, we declare, "Tired of arguing, let 'em go." "Tired of arguing, I'm going." "Don't waste time trying to talk them out of it." "We tried that ministry back in the sixties. Didn't work then, won't work now." "All Methodist churches are dying." "Clergy are lazy."

Hope makes demands: will we stay out of step with God's resurrection reality?

Rather than risk failure, it's safer to say, "Why make an effort? I already know how this story ends."

No, you don't. God only knows.

Cynical criticism is not curious. Hope stands on tiptoes, expectant.

Hope is motivating, "Yes, we can." Cynicism is debilitating, "No, we can't." When clergy are labeled as "lazy," pastoral inactivity and chronic fatigue are often symptoms of clergy hopelessness.

John Wesley must have been the most hopeful of Anglican priests. Where else would Wesley have caught his cockeyed conviction that it was possible—given the right sort of preaching, small groups, and methodical practices—for ordinary, poorly educated, gin-drinking eighteenth-century English people to become saints?

Say to your followers, "Love your enemies and pray for those who harass you" (Matt 5:44), and you must be the most hopeful of saviors, unafraid to risk failure. If God is truly in Jesus Christ, reconciling the world to himself, then hopelessness is a sign of the stubborn refusal to believe that God cannot do any new thing or make a way when we thought there was none. Jesus Christ is God's determination not to give up hope in us. No wonder Paul linked hope not only to love but also to faith (1 Cor 13), boldly claiming, "We were saved in hope" (Rom 8:24).

Giving up and leaving the UMC, as well as the attitude, "Let them go! I'm sick of their criticism and negativity!" could be cynicism spawned by hopelessness. How can either group be sure that it's not faithlessly impugning the ability of Jesus Christ to change hearts and minds?

Martin Luther King Jr. would have never written "Letter from Birmingham Jail" except out of his passionate, prophetic judgment upon the white church *and* his unquenchable hope in the power of Jesus Christ to save sinners. Thank God all those Black UMs who endured the indignities of last century's racialized Central Jurisdiction as well as our exclusionary clergy appointive system didn't give up hope for the predominately white UMC!

The hopeless don't write letters from jail cells in Rome or Birmingham, don't listen to sermons, and refuse to study the scriptures or to pray lest their hopelessness be rattled by the Holy Spirit. (That you risk reading this book suggests that in my harping on hope, I'm preaching to the choir.)

The church historically defined sloth as a sin of hopelessness. Sloth is not lazily lying too long in the bath; it's the arrogant failure to use the available means of God-given grace. Sloth is the temptation to believe that God is unwilling or unable to save sinners and to use them for God's purposes, a refusal to receive the sacraments, and to listen to sound teaching. Sloth is the passive-aggressive unwillingness to be loved by God or to be called to God's work.

On the Road with the Risen Christ

On the evening of the end of the worst week of their lives, two hopeless disciples trudged toward the village of Emmaus, talking about the trauma they had endured: their beloved Messiah, defeated, dead on the cross (Luke 24).

Suddenly they realized that a stranger walked alongside them.

"What are you talking about as you walk along?" the stranger asked.

Cleopas replied, "Are you clueless about what's happened in the last few days?"

"What things?"

"The death of Jesus of Nazareth! He did much good and was a great teacher. But prominent clergy and political big-wigs handed him over to be tortured to death."

Then Cleopas uttered those sad words: "We had hoped he was the one who would redeem Israel" (24:21). We had hoped!

Along the way, Jesus did Bible-Study-on-the-Go, opening up the whole Bible to them—Moses through the prophets. Still, the disciples were clueless. The exasperated teacher called them, "You foolish people!" and accused them of having "dull minds."

Jesus just can't help being truthful.

When they get to Emmaus, something in them bid the stranger to stay and share supper. There at table, when the stranger took, blessed, broke, and gave the bread, "their eyes were opened" (24:31) and they recognized Jesus. And though the risen Christ "disappeared from their sight," they marveled, "Weren't our hearts on fire when he spoke to us along the road and when he explained the scriptures for us?" (24:32). They raced back to Jerusalem, hopeless no more.

Take this as a parable of what happens in your church most Sundays. We gather, often fearful, sad, and hopeless. We can't see a way through our present situation. Then we open the scriptures and submit to God's word. In spite of our differences, we go together to the Lord's Table where bread is taken, blessed, broken, and given. Our eyes are opened, and not by us. We see. Jesus with us, even us. Full of hope not of our own devising, we race back into the world to tell everybody, "The Lord really has risen!" appearing to us, even us (24:34).

Where is Emmaus? Only those who break bread together in Christ's name know for sure.

Chapter 2
GOOD GRIEF

We're in a season of Methodist ending and loss. Christ's church has centuries of experience in leading folks through grief. Let's draw upon our bereavement expertise as we honestly acknowledge our church's losses before we think about what's next.

As a people convened by the announcement, "The Lord really has risen!" (Luke 24:34), we must consider that though Methodism as we have known it is ending, Methodism as God wants it may be just beginning. Fearful that death is what's next for your congregation? Take comfort: only God can plant or kill a church. Who knows? By God's grace, there may be hope for Methodism, supper at Emmaus all over again.

"I miss the funerals," I've heard retired clergy say.

When asked, "Why?" they respond, "More than at most times in ministry, I felt most needed when people were experiencing their greatest loss."

"The bishop can appoint you to a church," quipped a seasoned preacher, "but you're not really their pastor until you've shown that you can lead a difficult funeral."

A man once said, "My doctor, best friends, even my wife won't talk about my dying. Only my preacher has the guts to have an honest conversation about what's next."

Though tough, unwanted, and never welcomed, bereavement and the church's expertise with death and dying offer pastors and congregations an opportunity for a fresh encounter with the One who taught that resurrection is preceded by dying (John 12:24). Though death may be the "last enemy" (1 Cor 15:26), the only One ever raised from the dead has decisively dealt with our dying, making even the worst grief bearable.

Being compelled to say a word of hope at a funeral makes me a better preacher. Funeral sermons force me to dig deep. Put up or shut up time for believers. Either publicly testify to what Christians defiantly believe or else look silly as we babble sentimental bosh that everybody else already believes.

Grief disorients people. Old habits, comfortable daily rituals, and reassuring certainties crumble, and mourners are desperate for somewhere to stand, a reason to go on. Grievers confront the loss of the beloved, along with absence, aloneness, and intimations of their own mortality. Loss is the hard part of being human, the price we pay for loving. No wonder that bereavement often generates lies, sentimental fantasies, and self-deception ("She will live on in our memories," "This isn't a time to grieve; it's a time to tell jokes about our departed buddy and celebrate life.").

Still, no matter how we try to sidestep, death is a reckoning. What lasts? Has my life been for naught? What next? And the question behind the others, *Wherein is hope?*

Grief makes everybody a theologian. Our petty moralism, cheerful humanism, and self-help tips and tricks collapse before the specter of mortality. In death, there's no reasonable way not to think about God; only God has a future. Nothing about us is built to last. Confrontation with human morality and finitude forces us to rely upon God to do for us what we cannot do for ourselves. Driven to the core of our faith, we are made to admit that, if there isn't a God who loves to raise the dead, a crucified Savior who knows how to make a way when we thought there was none, then in death, we are without hope.

The purpose of our rituals of bereavement is transitional: to get the dead where they ought to be and the living where they need to be. Funerals are often consumed with looking back and retrieval of memories. Still, the living can't only look back but must also move forward. "What's next?"

Sure, we pastors care for the grieving, but we do so *in the name of Christ*. Because of Christ, pastors are able, even in a death-denying culture, to speak the truth in love (Eph 4:15), and congregations find the wherewithal honestly to acknowledging loss, while asserting a true hope that's more substantial than merely wishful thinking. Or, as Paul put it: we don't "mourn like others who don't have any hope" (1 Thess 4:13).

Loss Leading to Gain

Already, at the dawn of the church, in order to keep up with Jesus, Christians couldn't look back. The Letter to the Hebrews exhorts, "run the race that is laid out in front of us, since we have such a great cloud of witnesses surrounding us. Let's throw off any extra baggage, get rid of the sin that trips us up, and fix our eyes on Jesus, faith's pioneer and perfecter" (Heb 12:1-2).

The race we run is not necessarily the one we would have chosen; it's "the race that is laid out in front of us." Laid out by whom? A changing culture? Mandates from the General Conference? Institutional decline? Or by a God who loves to go on ahead?

Our past can be a resource for the present because we are cheered on by "such a great cloud of witnesses surrounding us." Still, some of our past may be "extra baggage" that we need to "get rid of." Can it be that some of our memories are "sin that trips us up"? We've got to fix "our eyes on Jesus," the pioneer who's always out ahead of us (Mark 10:32).

I hear many of the patterns of individual grieving in the current corporate grief of Methodist congregations and their pastors. As an experienced Grief Work Manager (aka, United Methodist Pastor with something like five hundred funerals behind me and my own looming before me), I offer here grief work for you and your congregation in order to enable the dead to get where they need to be and the living where they need to be in our church:

- Name your losses, your sadness in saying good-bye to what you've loved about the pre-COVID, pre-graying, pre-separation UMC. We will take some organizational hits, particularly our clergy. If you received your sense of self-worth, professional standing, job security, and community from the connectionalism of the old UMC, you have the most to grieve. Lifelong friendships are bound to be broken, in spite of our best intentions.

- Admit that much of our clergy grief is not shared by everyone in the church. Many are glad to be over and done with the aspects of church for which I'm grieving—publishing house, seminaries, camps, colleges, clergy talking shop after Annual Conference sessions, the Board of Global Ministries.

- Don't deny, rush, but—above all—don't avoid your grief. ("Accentuate the positive," "Keep doing what worked in the past as if nothing happened," "Let's talk about what's right with our church rather than what's wrong," can be forms of death-denial, lying about loss.)

- People in the crisis of loss tend to be narcissistic, turn inward, and become excessively self-concerned. Are we expending (wasting?) too much energy in organizational self-concern, either shoring up the UMC as it is (preoccupied with clergy issues, pensions, ordination, etc.) or in tinkering with the machinery to build a new denomination (at a time when people have given up on denominations)? Beware when the Archives and History room is the most attractive space in your church. The best antidote for the temptation to fuss over intramural matters is hands-on engagement in Christ's mission. More about that later.

- Grief provokes a crisis of identity. "Now I've lost who I thought I was going to be, who am I?" A crisis of identity demands a redefinition of purpose.

  "I don't want to spend the rest of my life as 'Widow Smith,'" she said with a tone of healthy defiance. "I can't let my dear husband's death define me."

  Mourners must imagine their lives after loss.

- It's aptly called grief work. Mourners ought not sit alone in silence; they need to move, to get out, and connect with the living. Even to those who mourn and would like nothing better than to be consumed by their grief, Jesus still says, "Follow me."

- Loss tends to be ambiguous. By the redemptive work of God, in even the saddest losses, something may be gained. "Unless a grain of wheat falls into the earth and dies, it can only be a single seed. But if it dies, it bears much fruit" (John 12:24). What I experience as UMC loss, the Global Methodist Church counts as gain.

- Many congregations are using their people and financial resources to keep a large, mostly empty building open or to pay the salary and benefits of a full-time pastor. If these congregations at last decide that their life-support measures are not fulfilling Christ's purposes and ought to be terminated or reconfigured, is that loss or gain?

- In the pain of the loss of what they've loved, sometimes mourners are angry, embittered, and fearful. They react to well-meaning friends' expressions of sympathy with resentment. Pastors and church leaders be warned: if you dare to wade into Methodist loss and urge movement beyond grief, you'll stir up resistance and hostility from some.

- In grief, you learn that some people are more helpful than others. Well-meaning friends, though they think they know what you are going through, don't. On the other hand, some may say things that you don't want to hear but, though painful, are helpful. They've dared, in friendship, to say what you dared not say to yourself.

As pastors, we have seen people crushed, defeated by tragedy and misfortune. Their defeat is understandable, a testimony to how much they cherished what they've lost.

Yet we have also walked with people through the "darkest valley" (Ps 23:4) and watched the resurrected Christ bring life out of death. I've seen them regroup, reframe, put on blue dress and makeup, get going even when that's the last thing in the world they felt like doing, stand at the funeral and sing Easter songs as if their lives depended on it, reorient themselves and start over as if they had not lost but gained.

When I complimented her on her amazing work in the congregation's food pantry, she said, "I thought my life was over, after Jim's death. Who would have guessed? Maybe this was the life God meant for me in the first place."

Of Christ's redemptive work, I am a witness. In my listening in preparation for writing this book I've moved from anger to despair, great grief and sorry cynicism, to gospel-induced hope and expectation. As the General Conference in Tampa rolled over and died, just after the Conference miraculously agreed upon a conciliatory plan to move forward, only to have that plan trashed by a quick ruling of the Judicial Council, I gave up hope for anything of help arising from the mechanisms of the general church. Then, the special General Conference in St. Louis debacle. The final nail in the coffin? The ill-considered "Protocol."

The week I lambasted the "Protocol," a former student said, "I was surprised that you lamented. Looks like you are about to get what you want."

What? "I don't want the UMC to split," I said.

"You've spent much of your life throwing rocks at the outdated, unproductive structure of the UMC, the legalistic *Discipline*, bumbling Boards and Agencies," he explained. "You're about to get your wish. All of that is being dismantled. Rejoice!"

When I upbraided a former student for leading his congregation out of the denomination he said, "You've dared to criticize the mechanism of the church that most bishops feel compelled to excuse or defend. How come Christ can't work even denominational division to his advantage?"

The coup de grâce to my grief was delivered by a young pastor who asked beguilingly, "With which aspect of the current

UMC are you most unhappy? God's plucking up and destroying or God's planting and creating?"

Jesus told a parable about an unproductive fig tree. Three years, no figs. In exasperation, the master ordered, "Cut it down!" (Luke 13:6-9). Is that our story? Or is our moment best characterized by the sower who slings seed with abandon only to be surprised by a miraculously fruitful harvest (Matt 13:1-9)?

As we lament the passing of the church we once knew, let's remind ourselves that God is an iconoclast. "You must have no other gods before me" (Exod 20:3) is the basis of all divine commands. God loves us enough to keep dethroning our idols and casting down our false gods. Whenever we've made even God's church into an adorable idol (or we've overthrown the church we had in order to create one more to our tastes), God has overturned our beloved idol and raised up a church more willing to do God's bidding. So, it's always possible, even in our worst grief to ask, "Is some of our loss God-wrought?"

Christians believe that death isn't the worst thing that can happen to you. Worse is never to have lived, or to live as if the significance of our lives is solely up to us. In the present moment we pastors must do more than pump life into a flagging institution; we need also to lead funerals for ministries and institutions that deserve a decent burial.

> Look! I'm doing a new thing;
>> now it sprouts up; don't you recognize it?
> I'm making a way in the desert,
>> paths in the wilderness (Isa 43:19)

By the way, if you are *not* in grief, rejoice, although you may be deceiving yourself. Still, not all grieve the losses being suffered by the UMC. Some see this not as a season of loss and death but of pruning that could lead to greater fruitfulness. I've interviewed dozens of Episcopalians/Anglicans, Southern Baptists/Cooperative Baptists, Presbyterians CA/Presbyterians CUSA about their experiences of denominational divorce. While some continue to lament "what we left behind," including beloved benevolent institutions, church buildings and graveyards, and dear friends, I've also heard many say, "There's life after the split." "Not as many will leave as you fear." "You'll be fine sooner than you think." "Some separate and then, after a while, come crawling back."

Are they deceiving themselves about their sad separation? God only knows.

We Can't Go Back

Walloped by the present, fearful of the future, the temptations to look back are manifold: "Remember the seventies? Sunday school was filled back then," so they say. "We were socially significant in the sixties, at the forefront of Civil Rights, right?"

I know someone who, ten years after her husband's death, carefully keeps his clothes in the closet, as if he's still there. Stuck in grief, she has given death more than is due.

"She will live on in our memories" is false consolation. Cherish your memories, commemorate key moments of the relationship that you lost, pray that you'll be granted grace to forgive those who wronged you, but you can't go back. No way but forward, particularly if you're trying to keep up with a living God.

Some pain remains, lessons are learned, memories are cherished and lovingly recalled. And yet, grief must not have the last word. The living must go on. After the church helps the dead get to where they need to be comes the hard work of getting the living to where they need to be.

"Preacher, just to keep you posted, I went by Mary's house this morning. Eleven o'clock, she comes to the door in her bathrobe and nightgown. Day half over! So I says to her, 'Mary, when are you planning to get dressed? I wanted us to have lunch together.'

"She tells me, in this shaking voice that she doesn't want to go anywhere. Then she starts crying. So I say, 'Look. Put on that pantsuit you bought when we were in Atlanta. Joe's funeral was a month ago and while we all miss him, you've got to get out and about. I want to tell you about the trip you are joining us on this fall. Widows in Washington. Now get moving!'"

How brash of the church to say to grieving people: get dressed, come to church (even when you may be angry with God at the moment), take a seat down front (an example to everybody), stand up and sing Easter hymns (even when you don't feel like singing), repeat the words of the creed (though you're not in a believing mood), and listen to the words of scripture (even when right now you don't want anybody to tell you anything). Allow your fellow members of the Body of Christ to help you back from loss to life.

A vignette from Jesus's ministry is illustrative:

> As Jesus and his disciples traveled along the road, someone said to him, "I will follow you wherever you go."
> Jesus replied, "Foxes have dens and the birds in the sky have nests, but the Human One has no place to lay his head."
> Then Jesus said to someone else, "Follow me."
> He replied, "Lord, first let me go and bury my father."
> Jesus said to him, "Let the dead bury their own dead. But you go and spread the news of God's kingdom."
> Someone else said to Jesus, "I will follow you, Lord, but first let me say good-bye to those in my house."

Jesus said to him, "No one who puts a hand on the plow and looks back is fit for God's kingdom." (Luke 9:57-62)

Here's Jesus being either uncharacteristically insensitive or very much Jesus. Doesn't scripture teach that we should honor our forebears (Exod 20:12)? To one in great grief over the death of his dear father, our Lord replies, "Let the dead bury their own dead"? Forbidding a farewell to the folks at home, Jesus pronounces as unfit for the kingdom anybody who "looks back." I could have made Luke 9:62 the proof text for this book were I not more sensitive than Jesus to people's pain.

Jesus won't allow us to stay forever at the funeral because (as I read Luke 9:57-61) participation in the mission of Jesus Christ eclipses even our loss and grief. Home is good. Honoring the ancestors? Fine. Family? I love mine. Yet Jesus says his mission to announce and enact God's kingdom is more important even than these otherwise good things. Don't look back.

The way we Methodists can deal with loss is to do our grief work and then to look for possible gains. We're not leading after a crisis; we are leading out of a crisis. Don't ask "How should we have handled things differently?" but rather, "How can we be better because of this?" Ecclesiastes says it's foolish to ask, "How is it that the former days were better than these?" (Eccl 7:10). Don't look back.

A Texas preacher told me that a wise cotton farmer told him that to plow a straight furrow, the farmer's eyes must be fixed on a point toward the horizon. "If you look back to see how straight you're plowing, you're sure to wobble and plow a crooked row." Jesus, at his parabolic best, couldn't have said it better. Don't look back.

I know an evangelical pastoral theologian who wrestled for years with what the Bible says (and doesn't say) about same-sex relationships. He spent hours in conversation, read books, and prayed. When God eventually led him to believe that same-gender love does not have to be contrary to Christian love, he was immediately terminated by his seminary, declared "mentally ill" by some of his peers, and lost many longtime friends.

"Eventually I got over my hurt and anger. Only took the Holy Spirit ten years to do it," he said with a laugh. "Jesus blessed those who mourn and promised us that one day he'd give us laughter. I loved my former life, my friends, the work I was doing for the church. But I had to move on if I was going to keep participating in Christ's work. I wanted to quit, but the Lord kept telling me, 'Don't put your hand to the plow and look back.'"

I hope my friend will stay Methodist. Whether or not he finds a Methodist church that's ambitious enough to welcome him, I'm sure he will stay in mission with Jesus.

We Don't Want to Go Back

"I do this one thing: I forget about the things behind me and reach out for the things ahead of me. The goal I pursue is the prize of God's upward call in Christ Jesus" (Phil 3:13-14).

I was ordained into the ministry of the ten-million-member United Methodist Church on a summer evening in 1971. The next morning, we began losing members. People were not walking away from the UMC in a huff; they were dying out. We had stopped making new Methodists and starting new congregations. We tinkered with denominational machinery but made no major changes in the way we did church, trained and deployed clergy, or governed our congregations. Every few years the bishops or

General Conference came up with a new quadrennial theme. The decline continued, even increased.

Studies indicated that when people actually left our church for another, our transfers were more active than the new members we received. Folks who were looking for increased church engagement tended to leave us; those who wanted a respite from their more demanding, usually more evangelical congregation, found the UMC a comfortable, moderate place to rest. Unknowingly, we gave people a theology that rationalized their disengagement from the church. We failed to retain our youth. If you grew up United Methodist, the chances of your being UMC by the time you were thirty were something like one in five. We began closing congregations at the rate of ten a week. Our median age rose to where it is today, perilously close to 65. The percentage of non-white UMC's declined, despite our hypocritical declarations of open hearts, open minds, open doors. Our puffed up "Making Disciples for the Transformation of the World" sounded hollow; we were neither making many disciples (read the numbers) nor (have you noticed?) transforming the world.

So, if someone says, "I wish we could go back to Methodism before the pandemic," or before the culture wars of the 1980s, or before Black Lives Matter, or before the January 6 insurrection, or before *Good News* became openly separatist, or before our debate about sexual orientation, you can respond, "Who would want to go back to that?"

Before a group of seminarians, I lamented the diminishment of some of our cherished Methodist institutions. "You can't serve the church that I served (and worked to my professional advancement, ha, ha). Sad to say, Methodism is dwindling."

A student piped up, "Are there actually students here at the Divinity School who pray, 'Lord, make me politically savvy enough so that one day I can be a delegate to General Conference'? Anybody here reading the weekly emails from the Board of Church and Society? If that's the reason they're going into the ministry, they're sick."

Most church leaders I have talked to agree: the pandemic and our threatened divisions didn't cause our current predicament; they exposed and exacerbated problems that we have been unable to manage for decades. If there had not been a pandemic, we would still be losing Methodism as we have known it. If there were no threatened division of our church, we would have the same work before us that's required to be part of Christ's mission.

Here's good news: *Your congregation is God's solution to all of our denomination's problems*. None of the dilemmas of the UMC can be solved by any agency, council, committee, or campaign outside of your congregation. Here's the bad news: Your congregation is God's solution to all of these problems.

In the past four decades when we've conceived of our Methodist future as a call for general church reorganization, we failed. You are now free to take responsibility for analyzing, diagnosing, strategizing, and implementing a Methodist future right now, right here with those whom God has convened in your congregation.

The rest of this book shows you how.

Saved in Hope

It's a rare funeral when Romans 8 fails to appear. Paul's unconditional affirmation that "nothing can separate us from God's love in Christ Jesus our Lord" is made for mourners. Yet Paul wrote these comforting words not for a funeral but rather to an imperiled, contentious congregation. Reading between the lines, I expect that First Church Rome was in a time of uncertainty, not knowing which step to take next, wondering if they were at the end of the road. They couldn't see into the future. Is there any hope for us as a church?

How does Paul respond to their plight? With some of his pushiest, most exuberant, sweeping assertions of faith (Rom 8:24-37). First, Paul urges patience, reminding the Romans that it's of the nature of hope not to be able to see clearly that in which we hope: "We were saved in hope. If we see what we hope for, that isn't hope. Who hopes for what they already see? But if we hope for what we don't see, we wait for it with patience."

Then Paul invokes the Holy Spirit as active precisely in those moments when hope is in short supply: "The Spirit comes to help our weakness. We don't know what we should pray, but the Spirit himself pleads our case with unexpressed groans. The one who searches hearts knows how the Spirit thinks, because he pleads for the saints, consistent with God's will."

Should we pray that the UMC will remain intact as it is? Ought we entreat God to give us an amicable separation? Should we pray that Methodists will be more welcoming to all Christians no matter their sexual orientation?

Although we aren't sure for what we ought to pray, it's comforting to know that the Spirit "pleads our case," praying that our prayers will be "consistent with God's will." Because of the Spirit's help, we don't have to pray, make decisions on controversial issues, lead or be the church alone.

Note that Paul urges patience and speaks of hopefulness, not on the basis of his conviction that the Romans have the right stuff to make it through the present uncertainty, but because he is convinced that, though we don't know everything we'd like to know about the future, we do know for sure "that God works all things together for good for the ones who love God, for those who are called according to his purpose." Knowing that God will never let us go is powerful comfort in our times of loss. Because of who God is and what God is up to, we can never be lost to God.

> Who will separate us from Christ's love? Will we be separated by trouble, or distress, or harassment, or famine, or nakedness, or danger, or sword? [church fights, shrinking attendance, flagging finances, difficult parishioners of the political right or the left, boorish bishops, self-righteous prophets, pedantic seminary profs, or cowardly clerics]?… I'm convinced that nothing can separate us from God's love in Christ Jesus our Lord. (Rom 8:24-37)

Whenever there's death, loss, and lament, preachers like Paul seized the opportunity defiantly to assert Christ's indomitable love.

Jesus told even a grieving son to get beyond his loss and "Follow me" (Matt 8:22). Jesus cares for and comforts us by calling us, yes us, to participate in his mission of salvation of humanity. "Nothing shall separate us" not only from the love of Christ but also from the call and claims of Christ. Go ahead, grieve our losses, institutional and personal, but don't allow your grief to paralyze you and rob you of your role in Christ's unfolding mission. Even amid our separations, loses, fears, and grief we live under his call and command, "Follow me."

Chapter 3
HOPE FOR CONGREGATIONS

What a sad group, gathered there on the evening of Day One (John 20:19-23). Jesus—their hope and trust—had been cruelly, humiliatingly, publicly tortured to death. They had hoped he would bring their redemption and liberation. But hope ended when Jesus was crushed under the heel of the authorities, political and religious, betrayed not only by the fickle crowd but by his own disciples. Now they huddled in darkness "behind closed doors because they were afraid." Why shouldn't they fear? The same murderous authorities who had crucified Jesus could now be searching for Jesus's followers.

There, as they trembled fearfully "behind closed doors" "Jesus came and stood among them." Jesus, the one whom they had forsaken in his time of trial, showed up to them in their grief, standing among those who didn't know how to stand by him.

Jesus greets his astounded followers, not with accusation and scolding, which they all deserved, but with his gracious, forgiving, "Peace be with you," which none deserved.

"He showed them his hands and his side," just to prove who he was—Jesus, the resurrected, is also the crucified. And the once despondent, grieving disciples "were filled with joy."

To make sure they heard, "Jesus said to them again, 'Peace be with you,'" disturbing their mourning.

And then Jesus's most astounding statement: "As the Father sent me, so I am sending you."

To those who repeatedly misunderstood, forsaken, and betrayed him, huddled together in fear behind locked doors, Jesus says, "As the Father sent me, so I am sending you." *Us?*

"Then he breathed on them and said, 'Receive the Holy Spirit. If you forgive anyone's sins, they are forgiven; if you don't forgive them, they aren't forgiven.'"

Upon these disheartened disciples, lamenting their loss, Jesus bestows his Holy Spirit in order to empower them for his mission of forgiveness. What is forgiveness but the gift of a future, the ability to go on in spite of one's grief about the past? Don't look back.

Earlier, when Jesus forgave a penitent woman, critics scoffed, "Who is this person that even forgives sins?" (Luke 7:49). Now Jesus gives his disciples his Holy Spirit to do the very same divine work that characterized his mission. Or as Jesus put it, "Whoever believes in me will do the works that I do. They will do even greater works than these" (John 14:12). *Us?*

Grieving they may be, but Jesus forbids his followers safely to huddle behind their closed doors. After Jesus's crucifixion and resurrection, all who follow Jesus are now sent by Jesus, thrust into the world, driven by his disruptive, empowering gust of Holy Spirit, to do the same work he has done. His death-defeating, life-giving work is now theirs. His mission (Latin: *missio* means "sent") is theirs by his Easter evening commission.

If you are a Methodist Christian, that means that somehow the risen Christ found a way to barge in upon you, coming through whatever doors you tried to close, and breathed his Holy Spirit on you and sent you forth as his ambassador to the world. The circuit rider on horseback heading into the wilderness, clutching a Bible, hunched down determinedly against the wind and rain, is you.

As a Methodist congregation, you are a sign that the risen Christ has determined not to reign in the Kingdom of Heaven without us. Though fear may have caused some in your congregation to check the security system and bolt the locks, Christ will not allow safety to be the purpose of gatherings in his name. He assembles us in order to send us forth. Your congregation is his strategy for accomplishing his salvation of the world.

I think John 20 the risen Christ intruding upon his disheartened disciples, sending them forth into the world to do his work—is a parable for the present moment of Methodism. Are you and your congregation feeling a sense of loss? Regret? Grief?

In light of John 20:19-23, brace yourself. There is hope, Methodist, Christian hope because Jesus Christ not only offers hope; he commissions us to do hopeful work as confirmation of our hope. He shows up, picks the lock on our doors, breathes the Holy Spirit upon us, and assigns us work to do. Us, even us.

Fearful? Mourning? Jesus will gather you, breathe upon you, and send you out on his errands anyway.

We Are Gathered

We have our work cut out for us, not because we must come to agreement in our arguments about sexual orientation, the authority of scripture, or boundaries for bishops. Our task is difficult, not because close to 60% of young Americans say they can get along fine without connecting with any church. The true instigator of your congregation's discomfort is Jesus Christ. Our church is not ours. We don't get to decide whom we will forgive or with whom we'll be church.

Contentiousness in your congregation? Disagreements about the purpose and mission of the church? Otherwise genteel and decorous congregants showing their fangs? While it's true we live in a combative, quarrelsome age where political divides also afflict the church, it's important to see some of this trouble as an expected spinoff of Jesus Christ's wildly expansive notion of salvation.

A Savior who sets out to seek, find, and save the lost (Luke 19:10), who when criticized because of the company he kept at table smirked, "If you are well, you don't need a doctor" (Matt 9:12, paraphrased). "I've not come for good, respectable, Bible-believing, justice-advocating, biblical-world-view, holy living, moderate, Methodist, hypersensitive-to-other-people's-wounds church people. I've come for sinners, only sinners."

Or as Paul put it to one of his contentious, disagreeing and disagreeable, combative congregations, "You might be willing to die for a really, really good person but he shows his love for us in that he died only for bad people—us" (Rom 5:7, paraphrased).

Jesus got into all manner of difficulty, not because he refused to be married to a woman, nor because of questions about his orthodoxy or biblical interpretation. The chief charge against Jesus was that he saved those whom no one thought could be saved, whom no one wanted saved. "This man welcomes sinners and eats with them" (Luke 15:2).

Never once did Jesus command us to love the lovely, loveable, and loving. Never did he allow his disciples to waste time attempting to determine which sin was the worst or who to ban from discipleship. Marriage was of as little interest to him as democracy. Welcoming outcasts and saving sinners were his obsessions.

Jesus's determination to save sinners, only sinners, would be challenge enough for us sinners without Jesus's equally determined insistence to put those being-redeemed sinners in the church. Because of Jesus's peculiar definition of salvation, we must be saved as a group. His ministry begins with the formation of a band of disciples (Matt 4:18-22). Paul didn't go forth into the world asking Gentiles thoughtfully to consider his message and then come to a personal verdict upon the truth. Paul went about planting churches, calling them "The Body of Christ," Christ's bodily, physical presence in the world. So if anybody encounters the risen Christ, it will be through the ragtag, divinely contrived gathering otherwise known as church.

Christ fervently prayed that all of his followers (church) would "be one" (John 17:21) and commanded us to get along with one another. Yet, from the first, we've been unable fully to live up to his expectations, having so little in common except love for him.

In your church and mine, let's face it: we congregate because we've been assembled. Little wonder that, from the first, there was disputation.

A group of clergy were bemoaning the divisions in our congregations.

"Not mine," said one. "Never served a more loving, unified church. We're all on the same page."

Widespread resentment among the clergy there gathered.

"Well, Tom, if you've got a unified, harmonious congregation, then you have failed at evangelism."

Dispute, division, and differences may not be signs that we have fallen short of church but rather signs that we are actually living out Christ's wildly expansive corporate salvation.

Be honest. The most challenging aspect of being commissioned by Christ is to be gathered by Christ with those with whom we have little in common other than Christ. Whatever work Christ does in the world, he chooses to do it in concert with the unruly choir that he assembles. He comes to us, busting through our locked doors, breathes his Holy Spirit upon us, and commissions us to work with him *together*. Christ, the great delegator, the relentless congregator. Salvation in Christ is always as ensemble.

I'll be honest: The hardest part of being pastor is having to work with anybody Jesus Christ drags in the door. You tell me the truth: The tough part of being laity is having to listen to the unlikely ones whom Jesus Christ called to preach.

My fear is that at the last judgment, I'll not be condemned for my bad preaching but rather Christ will say, "Nice to see you, but where are the others I asked you to bring with you?"

Division is easy, a natural propensity in a culture of rugged individualism, consumerism, political factionalism, and self-protectiveness from discomforting truth. Togetherness is hard. Congregating requires empowerment from outside ourselves, not I "but Christ lives in me" (Gal 3:20). When Jesus interceded for us, he prayed not that we would bow to biblical authority, be orthodox or prophetic or even that we would be right. He begged God to make us one (John 17:21). "This is how everyone will know that you are my disciples, when you love each other" (John 13:35).

Christ's propensity to congregate his followers, to save and to deploy us together, means that you can expect differences and disagreements, arguments, and dissension. Be surprised when you are on the same page about anything other than Jesus. Differences in your congregation can be life-giving. Debate, listen, and expect to be corrected and thereby brought closer to Jesus by a fellow Christian who may not be your type.

How would I have grown and matured in my faith without the jostling and insight that I received from pesky preachers, contentious congregants, and quarrelsome colleagues whom God used to say things to me that I didn't want to hear?

I'm glad that Black United Methodists didn't walk away from the UMC, though our white-dominated church gave them ample reason to do so. I have not the resources, on my own, to confront my own racialized sin, nor do I have the means to self-pronounce forgiveness and release from it. I wish everyone who is thinking of bolting from the UMC would ask a Black Methodist, "Why did you not give up hope for the UMC? Who gave you the courage to stay?"

We claimed that the bonds that held the UMC together were theological; we learned that they were cultural, economic, and sociological. When those bonds break, so does the church. We felt unified because we congregated on the basis of common culture. When those cultural props were removed, we found we had trouble convening the church. There's no way Methodists can arrive at a political, ethical, ideological agreement that will end our divisions and make us whole. That's okay because consensus is not our reason for gathering. The sole source of togetherness: Jesus Christ has come through our locked doors, convened us, breathed upon us, and sent us forth in mission.

If our church divides, then we say to a polarized America, "We're no better than you. Christ gives us no means of being in fellowship with those with whom we disagree." Not a very compelling witness, that.

My ideal church member is that person who is able to love Christ enough to say to me, "While I don't agree with you (as best I understand your stance from your rather incoherent sermons), since Jesus Christ has brought us together (without giving either of us much choice in the matter) and then commanded us to stay together (even though it would be easier to keep to ourselves), I'll keep talking, continue listening, and keep praying that we will grow more committed to Christ—*together*."

When it comes to being Christian, it's better to be in relationship than to be right. Or as John Wesley put it, "Christianity is a social religion. To turn it into a solitary thing is to destroy it."

Be fair. Think what you are asking of people when they join a church: to believe that there's a gathering more important than their nation, their political party, or even their family, to give money for the needs of perfect strangers, to stay in conversation with those who are put off by their politics, to receive the gospel of God from the hands of another who may not be their type.

It's so much easier to leave than to stay. Little wonder that more people exit, not for another denomination, but to leave church altogether.

In recent years the one who said, "I've been a Methodist all my life," began to shop around for a church that "meets my needs" and to take a walk when the congregation turned out to be different from the church that was purchased. The congregation became a retail outlet for spirituality, a dispenser of goods and services to savvy consumers who picked and chose the savior who most closely aligned with their values. We trained folks to ask,

"What's in it for me?" "What can you do for me and my family?" rather than, "What must we do to be saved?" (Acts 2:37).

Many people today are looking for help with marriage and family, belonging, community, but it's not certain that they are looking for the Jesus whom Methodists try to follow. False gods are always easier to get along with than the true, living God because false gods don't have to tell the truth. Besides, any god who meets all your expectations for God can never be a god who can forgive and save you.

"I can't believe you preached a whole sermon and not once stated explicitly, unequivocally your support for LGBTQ+ inclusion," a critic complained.

"The congregation knows me," I retorted. "It's not that full inclusion isn't important; it's that our church is in a mess partly because right-left, progressive-traditional, we love our cherished causes more than we've loved the continuance of the congregation. As an ordained leader, I'm commissioned to love togetherness more than my cause."

The general UMC was headed for dissolution when commitment to caucuses (Good News, The Confessing Movement, Reconciling Ministries, and so forth) trumped Methodists' love for the UMC.

I know a congregation where the pastor took a forceful, prophetic stand for the inclusion of all persons, regardless of their sexual or gender orientation—without working to bring her congregation along with her. "Full inclusion for all is an absolute right," she announced with prophetic adamancy. She led the crafting of a long Statement of Welcome and directed that it be read at the beginning of every Sunday's worship.

Today, her congregation has shrunk to the faithful few left over from the hard work of previous pastors. Her prophetic stance on inclusiveness appears to have resulted in the inclusion only of those who are white and over seventy.

Caucuses and causes are easier to lead than a church. Caucusing simplifies discipleship as we rally with people with whom we are already in agreement. No seminary training is required to be a leader of a caucus. Who needs a leader when all are willingly walking in the same direction?

Even if you leave the UMC for another denomination, I guarantee that, once you get to know your fellow church members, you will risk being in sermons or group discussions where you must ask yourself, "How much disagreement can I live with?"

"I just can't stay in a church where there are insensitive, uncaring people who say those things about my LGBTQ+ siblings." If you worship Christ in a congregation, you'll have to.

"I can't remain in any church that would ordain a lesbian bishop." Bet you can.

"Let these closed-minded traditionalists leave!" Make it safe for us open-minded.

Paul's injunction to forbear (put up with) one another in love (Col 3:13; Eph 4:2) ought to be tattooed on the biceps of every Methodist. How different might have been the disastrous 2019 General Conference if we had begun with the presiding bishop asking us to stand, raise our right hands, and repeat the words, "I promise to speak honestly, to listen carefully, and then *to put up with one another* no matter who offends me." Instead we wasted an entire first day with each secretly praying, "Lord, make my brothers and sisters agree with me on the one issue I think more important than our church."

46

We Are Gifted

I'm sure that The Letter to the Colossians was written (as just about all of Paul's letters) to a disunited congregation. The letter opens, not with talk about division, not by choosing up sides and debating who's right and who's wrong (rarely does Paul waste time citing the specific details of congregational disunity), not by arguing who's in and who's out (Paul is clear: all have sinned and all receive Christ's mercy, Romans 3:23-24). Colossians opens by singing of Christ the grand congregator:

> He made it so you could take part in the inheritance, in light granted to God's holy people. He rescued us from the control of darkness and transferred us into the kingdom of the Son he loves. He set us free through the Son and forgave our sins.
>
> The Son is the image of the invisible God,
> the one who is first over all creation,
>
> Because...all things were created through him and for him...all things are held together in him.
>
> He is the head of the body, the church...he reconciled all things to himself through him—
>
> whether things on earth or in the heavens.
> He brought peace through the blood of his cross. (Col 1:13-18)

I'm advocating for putting up with one another, togetherness, the courage to congregate, the continuance of Methodism, and the priority of your congregation, not simply for the survival of an institution I love and to which I am indebted, but because to the church, yes, the poor old church, your congregation and mine, has been given the truth about God. God really is in Christ reconciling the world to himself, bringing all things together. How? Maybe not exclusively but certainly primarily through your congregation.

The church is not self-created and will ultimately be held accountable to a truth that the church doesn't produce. Christianity is a faith you can't tell yourself; you must receive Christ from the hands of another. Someone has got to tell you, live the faith before you in order for you to know Christ. Gift. Grace. The much-debated United Methodist "trust clause" has its basis in the recognition that if you are worshipping and serving in a church today, you are the recipient of the sacrifices, hard work, and investment of saints who came before you. We contemporary UMC leaders are only stewards who have been entrusted with the Lord's prized possessions. This ought to make those who speak of "It's our church and we can take it with us if we want," or those who boast, "They can't take our church," think twice. *Our* church?

At the same time, I'm thinking somber thoughts about the way in which the UMC, given to my safekeeping as a pastor and then as a bishop, has dwindled dramatically during my years of church leadership. What have *I* done or left undone that has made *me* an unwitting accomplice in the decline and division of the UMC? How did I allow myself to be consumed with internal denominational bickering rather than lead congregations in being salt and light to the world?

The church never claimed that the corporately embodied good news will make your life more livable (Jesus suggested that it wouldn't) or that you'll find that congregating is a helpful technique to be happy. The contention is that congregating is how a crucified and resurrected savior has chosen to save the world and that your participation in his church is how Christ saves you.

Chapter 4
METHODISTS MOVING OUT IN MISSION

Desperate to revive a dwindling congregation, I secured the services of a renowned church consultant who spent two days talking with every congregational leader, studying our metrics, and then reported on what we needed to do to have a future in our beloved, historic building. The leadership of the congregation enthusiastically embraced the consultant's recommendations.

As he departed the next morning, the consultant and I walked through the church's sanctuary. He looked up at the huge stained-glass window over the door.

"What's that scene?" he asked.

"You're obviously not a Methodist," I said with a laugh, "That's an iconic moment from John Wesley's ministry. Refused access to an Anglican pulpit by a bishop who thought Wesley was nuts, Wesley stood on his father's tomb and preached to a group gathered in the cemetery. 'I don't need permission to preach in this parish,' scoffed Wesley, 'the world is my parish.'"

"My chief recommendation," said the consultant, "is to end every service by having your congregation turn and face that window. That image ought to be imprinted on their hearts every time they depart. They're Methodists; their mission isn't this building; it's the world."

Methodists indeed. Jesus didn't die for the church. He thinks the whole world is his. Thus John Wesley and his followers burst forth from the parochial established church and into the fields proclaiming, "Salvation for all!"

Your congregation's health before the pandemic and before the threat of separation is more determinative of your future than either the pandemic or separation. Eighty percent of all Methodist congregations are in decline and have been so for the last two decades. In studying four decades of UMC diminishment, we've found that *the single most influential factor in the life of a Methodist congregation is its external focus.*

Church as safe sanctuary has become a tempting alternative for congregations during the pandemic. As we come out of the pandemic, now is a good time to admit that church-as-sanctuary is less than church is called to be. The congregation as safe haven for hurting individuals seeking care makes church a refuge not only from stress but also from accountability to mission. Free-floating, do-it-yourself, vague "spirituality" becomes the purpose of church rather than equipment for discipleship—salvation detached from vocation, congregation severed from mission.

Pastors find it easier to run errands for an inwardly focused congregation; the congregation pays our salaries and internal pastoral care is less demanding than engaging God's people in God's mission.

When congregations or pastors confuse the purpose of the church as care and consolation of our church members, or as rallying around our prior agreement on various social issues, fidelity is measured by how many of our members are content with the present state of the congregation. This is church on its way out. Judging from Methodism's numbers, four fifths of our congregations are confused.

Call me simplistic, but I tell pastors to stand, before or between services, at the front door, or out in the yard or parking lot of the church so that they interact with people outside the building. That sends a signal to the congregation that the work of the church is inside out.

Many times have I heard, "Though we're not growing, we are a caring, loving congregation."

Sorry, that's not good enough for Jesus.

Inwardly focused, all-on-the-same-page comity, internal congregational maintenance can be accomplished by sincere, dedicated people led by a loving, caring pastor. No God needed to help create a warm, caring club of like with like. Only when a congregation focuses on mission outside itself, must it rely upon Christ for help.

Made for Mission

In the spring of 1739, George Whitefield wrote John Wesley that the crowds coming to hear him preach were so great that he needed help. Wesley, Anglican, Oxford don, was horrified that Whitefield should ask him to engage in unorthodox street preaching.

On Saturday, March 31, Wesley relented and went to Bristol where he "submitted to be more vile" and preached in the open air. Preaching on the Sermon on the Mount, he noted that Jesus preached his greatest sermon in a field, even though many synagogues were available. "I thought saving souls a sin if not in a church," Wesley reflected later. *Mission* is what happens when the gospel is taken over boundaries, the gospel going public, by word and deed, explained and enacted, to those who have not yet heard the news that God is taking back what belongs to God.

From the first, Wesley's Methodism was a "go to" rather than a "come to us" movement. Lots of churches practiced hospitality and welcome. Methodists—made for mission—were proactive, intrusive, and extroverted: we'll come to you.

Wesley looked upon England and saw, not a Christian nation but a mission field. The most helpful discovery in recent decades is that North America is a vast, unconverted, unreached mission opportunity. Being Christian is no longer the natural, cultural, American thing to be. This is no longer "our" world, if it ever were. Even we mainline protestant Methodists have become resident aliens in a culture we thought we owned. Now, you don't have to get on a plane to be a missionary; the mission field has become your neighborhood.

My parents never worried about whether I'd grow up Christian; it was the only game in town. One became Christian by osmosis, by being fortunate enough to be born in God-we-trust-America. "Christian" meant "American." Unable to tell the difference between a flag and a cross, school, home, and community served as props for the church. Who believes that today? There is a new awareness that the Christian life is not innate. If we are to persevere, if our children are to grow up Christian, there must be transformation and formation. Disciples are made, not born.

The future belongs to Methodist congregations who see our divestment and disestablishment by American culture as an opportunity to reclaim our rightful participation in the mission of Jesus Christ. Rescued from the heresy of making our mission the survival of the congregation, reborn as a people who listen and then respond to the voice of God, we've got news for a world that doesn't yet know it's God's until we show and tell.

Nineteenth-century Methodism swept across this continent as a movement of mission, blessed with a polity uniquely suited for the evangelizing of the American frontier. Our declension is a crisis of mission. When our church became the subject of its own story, ceasing to be the church for the world, inward rather than outward, checking one another out on our orthodoxy rather than going out into an unbelieving world, we ceased being God's instrument for God's mission in God's world. The mainline got sidelined.

Extroverted with Jesus

Don't let the current Methodist crisis of decline and fragmentation go to waste; see our present problems as a catalyst for joining Christ in mission. Not all mission engagement leads to growth. Some good practices lead to more interesting and authentic (faithful?), though not larger churches. And yet, it's hard to imagine growth that's not generated by a congregation's active participation in mission.

The most important innovation in church architecture in this century has been the welcome space. We once built our churches with small vestibules that led from the front door into the large worship area. No need for a big entrance space when we saw one another around town all week. A few decades ago, growing congregations realized that their welcome area needed to be a space that enabled the welcoming of strangers. Large spaces, well-illuminated, with comfortable seating, refreshments, and trained greeters became standard practice.

I know a church that changed the signs of its designated parking spaces from, "Our Senior Members" to, "Parents with Young Children." Extroverts.

"The worship experience begins in the parking lot," explained the Hospitality Leader of an expanding congregation. "Trained greeters roam the lots on Sunday morning. They greet, then hand off guests to our Worship Hosts at the front door. The Worship Hosts sit with them during the service and help them feel at home. After service, the Hosts invite them and then accompany them to our Guests Lunch where they can meet the worship leaders. The next week, the Hosts invite them back to our church." That's a remarkably different understanding of the church's context than fifty years ago when our attitude tended to be, "This is America. Christian is the American thing to do. We just open our doors. You'll worship God when, where, and how we say."

You'll know that your congregation is becoming more externally focused when you hear, "Let's try this and see if it connects with those in our neighborhood who haven't yet heard the good news."

Not, "How many Methodists live close by?" but, "How many unchurched people live in our neighborhood and how can we get to know them?"

"What gifts has God given this congregation that people in our neighborhood need?"

"What's God already doing in our neighborhood, and through whom? How can we hitch on?"

Rather than, "How can we get more people in church?" say, "If we succeed in getting our church out into the neighborhood, we'll get more people in church."

Institutions

When the "Nones" (29%, highest in American history) and "Dones" say that they don't like "institutional religion," they mean that they don't like congregating. Assembling as a congregation is the way Jesus has instituted his mission. "Body of Christ" is the peculiar institution required by Jesus's demanding "Follow me."

Lots of Americans are freestyling faith. Jesus without a Body. King without a kingdom. Many who have no interest in denominational, institutional separation have already separated in their consciousness, attempting to worship God online, or becoming infrequent, casual participants in the life of a congregation. They're attempting a feat unknown in Christian history: to pick and choose the church that "will meet my needs" or "heal my wounds" or "shares my values," or no church at all. Just what one would expect in an individualistic culture that glorifies individual choice as the hallmark of humanity. "I am who I choose to be." "My life is the sum of my choices." "I'll determine how Jesus loves me." "I control the communication between me and God." "I'll keep Jesus from making me uncomfortable."

Christianity, on the other hand, follows a Savior who said upfront, "You didn't choose me, but I chose you and appointed you so that you could go and produce fruit and so that your fruit could last" (John 15:16). We didn't get to select the God we got. Nor are we able to decide the life to which we are appointed. Any "god" whom I can freely choose can never be my God. Any life that I concoct through my own independent, free, individual choices is not the life worth living.

When the church is a club that you chose, on the basis of your assessment of your greatest needs, or your personal tastes and preferences, or current political orientation, then there's a good chance that you will have forfeited the opportunity for accountability, growth, and fresh adventure in your discipleship. One of the reasons why Christian discipleship is so demanding is precisely because you didn't choose Christ until after he had chosen you (Wesleyans call it "prevenient grace," God coming to you before you know it's God).

Pause a moment and meditate upon all the ways that your membership in your Methodist congregation was not your free, individual choice but was part of God's choice of you, God's gift, call it grace.

No human community exists without the gift of institutions. The Next Gen who attempts to fend off my evangelism with, "I'm just not into institutional religion," will, next Sunday, eat at a chain restaurant, blow an afternoon at an NFL game, and pay high tuition at a university like the one where I teach. Even to say, "I don't like institutions," is to show one's institutionalization into the ideology of North American, anti-institutional individualism.

No effective, sustained partnership in Christian mission is without institutions. A group with no mission beyond itself needs no institutionalization. Methodist clergy of all stripes who criticize the way the UMC is institutionalized find their antipathy evaporates when it comes to a bishop working them into a pastoral appointment, protecting their rights to due process, or benefiting from the clergy pension fund, none of which they invented.

The United Methodist Church is an institution in much the same way as the "institution of marriage" or Jesus's "institution" of the Lord's Supper. Marriage is a continuing institution based upon established traditions, customs, rituals, and common commitments that are renegotiated and adapted by a couple over time.

Nobody knows what they are getting into when they get married or what will be required to sustain the institution of their marriage. The Service of Christian Marriage therefore asks couples to make unconditional, open-ended promises to live together "for better, for worse, in sickness and in health," vowing to stay together no matter what, to find a way to live together "until death do us part." It's no good to plead (though I've had some parishioners try), "But I didn't know my husband would love pro football," or "I should have been warned that my wife would take up skydiving at forty." Argumentation, adaptation, and improvisation are required in order to keep a lifelong promise to "love, honor, and keep" one another.

When I urged a couple in my church, who had been living together, to take the plunge and submit to the promises of marriage, they asked, "But we already love one another. Why should we go through all that traditional, prescribed stuff and get married?"

I mustered my argument for the institution: "I'm always surprised by how the Service of Marriage doesn't say much about 'love.' The focus is on fidelity, public promises. You may be in love, you may be living together, having sex, but you have not made a public, lifelong declaration. You haven't sent that signal to your friends and family who could provide much-needed, long-term support for keeping your promises. Come on. Live dangerously. Make promises and I promise that God promises to help you keep them."

Even though The United Methodist Church is an institution in much the same way that marriage is an institution, alas, beginning in the 1960s, the UMC instituted rigid, top-down, overly articulated, legislated rules, procedures, and prohibitions. General Motors of the 1950s.

Which is only one more reason why your congregation can't look back to the general church and its mechanisms for help surviving and thriving into the future. Your congregation more closely resembles the way the Body of Christ is meant to be an "institution" than the way the *Book of Discipline* has tried to order the church in the last four decades.

In our first 100 years, Methodists institutionalized for mission. Our deployment of clergy, where we placed our churches, our rules and procedures, had relative clarity of purpose: *Mission*. We now need radically to right size the institution that has become an impediment to mission. Indeed, as I read the plans of the new breakaway denomination, I find much in which to rejoice in their proposed streamlining, cost-cutting, and simplification. Which makes me all the more sad that the UMC failed to make the necessary reforms that might have not only saved us from splintering but also made us a more active participant in Christ's mission. The worst I can say about The Global Methodist Church is that, institutionally it is a disappointing replication of some of the most problematic internal organization of the UMC.

Those who complain of the UMC being boringly "institutionalized religion" are right. Their criticisms of our legalism, poor management, waste, clergy dominance, and introverted dysfunction are well taken. Denominational Christianity, as a way of organizing the church, is on the way out. GMC, your big idea for righting what's wrong with a mainline denomination is to organize another mainline denomination? Seriously?

"Institute" in Latin means to set up, to order, but it can also mean to begin, to start new, which is what's appealing about making a new denomination. But will the separatists find that they are bedeviled by the same inward-looking organizational challenges as the UMC they're trashing?

Both the UMC and any denominational successor share the institutional problems of:

- dominance by one generation that is rapidly aging out

- bishops who don't know how to lead mission

- clergy dominance of church decision-making and direction

- church populated primarily by one race

- expensive, wrong-sized church buildings

- thousands of tiny, unsustainable congregations isolated from population centers

- attracting and keeping young clergy whose generation is suspicious of institutions

- attempting to form the church and oversee the clergy by legislative, rule-driven means

Some of this age's anti-institutionalism is the romantic, unrealistic desire for a Jesus without a body, adoration of a King without being a participant in his kingdom. Some pastors' anti-institutionalism is slothful reluctance to learn how to do the hard, essential, never-ending labor of institutional refurbishment. Still, if you're willing to undertake the tasks necessitated by Christ's mission mandate, read on!

Conflicted Christians

Sitting in my study the morning after a stormy church meeting, I asked myself, "What did I do wrong?" The Administrative Board had just shot down our plans for a community day care center at our church.

I should have moved more slowly. Why didn't I count the votes before allowing them to vote? Perhaps I should have used more scripture references in my presentation? Then, in prayer, the Holy Spirit spoke directly to me: *What about the word "cross" do you not get?*

Take Jesus's mission seriously, count on conflict. Nobody has ever found a way to follow crucified Jesus free of friction.

If indeed this is a conflicted, fractious time, your congregation is the best place for potentially quarrelsome, divisive conversations. What a gift to say, "Hi, I'm Will and I'm a biased, limited, frail sinner, so I expect that my sin infects my point of view, in ways of which I'm unaware, and I know that you are also a sinner whose views are similarly tainted by your sin. Now, let's have a no-holds-barred argument, and let's both try to listen well, to present our positions honestly and beguilingly, and to risk the possibility of modification of our positions but above all *let's promise together to go the Lord's Table and receive our Lord's body and blood no matter what.*"

If some subjects are disputed and anxiety-producing, then the pastor must curate conversations that, though conflicted, may be productive and helpful to the survival of the congregation. On the other hand, the pastor must also be willing to discourage those conversations where there is little likelihood of resolving differences through continued argument.

A sad aspect of our denominational splintering is the loss of interlocutors who see things differently than I. Their departure from our contentious conversations also encourages the non-Christian attitude that if I fail to get you to adopt my position, I'm free to plead exhaustion and leave the conversation.

Here's the thing: *Much of your congregation's current discomfort arises from your attempt to be faithful to the mission of Jesus Christ.* Jesus refuses to allow us to choose with whom we shall congregate. We know who is at the center of the Kingdom of God but we don't know the Kingdom's circumference. We can't designate whom Jesus saves. Or, as John Wesley put it, "Salvation for all!" With such expansive notions of God's grace, expect arguments, differences, and divisions in our congregating, and be surprised when everybody is on the same page.

I believe, with the UMC, that the Bible is God's authoritative word, the test of our fidelity, the rule of faith. Anyone who would set boundaries on the expanse of the Kingdom of God, placing barriers between Jesus and his determination that all be saved, any group that attempts to muster theological justification for sorting and then dividing and splitting a church will find scant scriptural support for their actions.

I received a manifesto from allegedly "traditionalist" Methodists working to remove their congregation from the UMC. The traditionalists announced they were separating due to their passionate obedience to "scriptural authority," creating a church that "saves souls rather than does social action. Refuses to recognize same-sex marriage or tolerate clergy who do. Loves and honors America." Which "scriptural authority" gave you that?

When the right person—who is just whom a congregation needs to lead it forward with Christ into mission—shows up for The Global Methodist Church but is deemed to be the wrong sexual orientation, or the right person shows up for the UMC who says, "I've got real problems with same-sex unions." What then? Be careful; this just might be a prompting by the Holy Spirit. You'll have to "test the spirits" (1 John 4:1), won't you? No way to do that without some friction.

We meet no fragmentation in the present church that's not prefigured in scripture. We have four Gospels (count 'em, four) when it would have been much simpler to have had one. Something about Christ—perhaps his wondrously rich and multifaceted divinity or maybe Christ's diverse and far-flung mission— required four witnesses to do justice to their subject. The church in its wisdom knew there was no way to have a unified, singular witness without silencing someone's witness. There's no way to unify your congregation and end disagreement without stifling or excluding someone's testimony to the complex truth of Christ.

Self-designated "traditionalists" have taken on a huge task. Christian tradition is rich, multifaceted, so much so that it's rarely self-evident just what part of our tradition commands the present moment. For instance, as today's church struggles with how to be more inclusive of fellow Christians and their diverse gender orientations, some "progressives" point to early Jewish Christians wrestling with the inclusion of Gentiles. At the so-called "Jerusalem Council" (Acts 15), the church formally, publicly stated that, no matter what much of scripture said, Christ's salvation extended beyond the bounds of Judaism. Yet "traditionalists" can cite the same passage, noting that while the early church made adaptations for wider inclusion, it did so conditionally, setting up some core, minimum standards for baptism (abstinence from food that had been offered to idols, sexual immorality, and eating animals that had been strangled, which includes everybody in my town). I dare contemporary Methodists to find guidance in that passage without interpretive debate.

And as for you proud "progressives," just what, in orthodox Christianity, have you enlightened modern folk progressed beyond? Surely you don't think that we, who have never been able to keep up with Christ, progress beyond him?

Why did conflict reach a fever pitch in the nascent church requiring the convening of the Jerusalem Conference: *Jesus.* "You will receive power when the Holy Spirit has come upon you." Why? So that "you will be my witnesses in Jerusalem, in all Judea and Samaria, and to the end of the earth" (Acts 1:8). No way for First Church Jerusalem to stay true to its traditional, foundational purpose without adaptation and creative reconfiguration in response to what the Holy Spirit was up to.

If your expectation for church is placidity, serenity, and stability, this will be a tough season. On the other hand, if you have allowed your need for self-protective, all-affirming, graciousness to limit the boundaries of your church, you may discover the wonder of being the Body of Christ even with those with whom you disagree.

Try to finish the statement, "As those who are forgiven, saved, and commissioned by Christ, we ought to..." You will quickly discover the diversity of ways that Christ reveals himself to his people, the complexity inherent in a truly human/truly God Savior, and the conflict that comes when you realize that

Christ has chosen to speak to others in ways that he has not spoken to you.

Your congregation can be an impediment to mission or a gift of God for generating creativity among its members, nurturing the young, attracting and inculcating new members, a safe place for difficult conversations, a primary location for life-changing encounters with a living God, a source of courage for standing with Christ against the wiles of the world, and for identifying and preparing leaders of the institution that give it a future.

The ninety-and-nine sheep were all too happy to let the one lost sheep wander—hard to get along with, kept asking embarrassing questions, harping on same gripes, and voted for an adulterous casino owner for president. You know the type. One of them.

But as for the shepherd, well, you know the story.

What's Next?

The New Testament ends with The Revelation to John, a strange, wonderful vision of the ending of an old world and the beginning of a new, of the fulfillment of God's promised restoration of God's intent for all creation and the successful completion of God's mission to have a "new heaven and a new earth" (Rev 21:1). The Greek word translated as "revelation" is *apokálypsi*, "unveiling," "disclosing."

When we appear to be losing the Methodism that many of us have loved and we're not clear about the new Methodism to be born, we shouldn't be surprised that biblical apocalyptic has resonance. Toward the end of Luke's Gospel, as Jesus resolutely heads toward the cross, Jesus goes apocalyptic (Luke 21:5-28).

Jesus and his disciples were walking by the temple one day, admiring the "beautiful stones and ornaments dedicated to God." What a beautiful building! How glorious, historic, and eternal!

Jesus said, "As for the things you are admiring, the time is coming when not even one stone will be left upon another. All will be demolished."

"There will be great earthquakes and wide-scale food shortages and epidemics. There will also be terrifying sights and great signs…. They will take you into custody and harass you because of your faith." Batten down the hatches. There's a storm a-comin', the world's response to the salvation it doesn't want.

Don't look back at the temple's faded glory, look forward to the glory that is to be revealed. The worst of times for the temple admirers and defenders Jesus describes as the best of times for witness: "This will provide you with an opportunity to testify."

Don't bother with sermon preparation or "prepare your defense in advance. I'll give you words and wisdom that none of your opponents will be able to counter or contradict."

Bad news: "You will be betrayed by your parents, brothers and sisters, relatives, and friends…. Everyone will hate you because of my name." Then good news: "By holding fast, you will gain your lives."

Jesus concludes his apocalyptic promises and warnings with joyful reassurance: "Now when these things begin to happen, stand up straight and raise your heads, because your redemption is near" (Luke 21:28).

Take just a moment and ask what witness God may be asking of your congregation in this apocalyptic time. Is this parable for you?

Chapter 5

THE BODY OF CHRIST IN MOTION

John Wesley said that Methodism was driven by "practical divinity," theology meant to be practiced, embodied, and enacted. Though a fine enough preacher, Wesley is best remembered as a brilliant strategist who boldly instituted new forms of church in service of mission.

Young Methodism nearly died in the new United States after the American Revolution. Who wants to be part of a royally established church? Creative strategists like Francis Asbury, more radical innovator than Wesley, made Methodism a fecund mission movement that evangelized the unchurched new nation. Our task is more akin to Asbury's bold birth of a new church than Wesley's lay reform of an established church.

Why are there more UMC churches than US post offices? Methodist Circuit Riders didn't just present individuals with an interesting message; they formed congregations in thousands of places other Christian groups refused to go.

From the first, Methodists hoped that every church is the Body of Christ in Motion. The Wesleyan warmed heart bears fruit in active, hands-on service.

Let's get practical.

Six Challenges

Though these are uncertain times, we don't have to wait for certainty to gain clarity about the way forward. Whether or not your church is thinking about leaving the UM connection, no matter how well or poorly you've regrouped after the pandemic, your congregation probably needs:

1. Clarity about your congregation's part in God's mission

2. Vision of where God wants you to go from where you are presently most comfortable

3. Strategies for overcoming introversion by reaching and serving the surrounding community

4. Tactics for reaching, integrating, and equipping new disciples

5. Simple and accelerated decision-making and ministry follow-through

6. Active, resourceful leadership from the pastor as mission leader

Address these six challenges or you'll be dead in the water.

As bishop, I was frustrated with the stodginess, endless process, and overly complex bureaucratic machinery of my Annual Conference. Then it hit me: everything that needed to happen in our Conference—simplification of decision-making and execution, focus on mission rather than meetings, pulling the plug on non-productive ministries—had already been done in every vibrant, growing congregation in my Conference. I began regular meetings with pastors in those congregations, attempting to learn how to initiate change in my Conference that had already been accomplished in their churches.

So here's some good news: you don't have to wait for General Conference finally to meet, yearn for guidance from the Council of Bishops, or see if a new denomination gets off the ground. No *Book of Discipline* revisions are needed. Seek not majority vote approval by your congregation. Go ahead, tackle these six challenges.

No mission other than internal congregational happiness and contentment? Choose up sides and fight over matters that are extrinsic to Christ's reconciliation of the world. If there is conflict in your congregation and internal wrangling over social issues, it's probably because your congregation has ignored the six challenges. Doctrinal squabbling tends to be low in congregations whose commitment to mission is high, not because of their laissez-faire attitude toward biblical authority, but due to their commitment to theology as practical mission strategy.

I know a pastor who fancied himself as "traditionalist" in regard to questions of sexual orientation. When his dwindling congregation finally got serious about mission to their neighborhood, the people they reached compelled him to rethink church.

"It was like the Acts 8 all over again," he said. "I got to play Philip. Maybe these newcomers, many of whom appear to have a sexual orientation different from mine, weren't wrong when they got the wild notion that Jesus wants them to be Methodists no matter what some Methodists think of them."

I don't have answers for your congregational context. All I know is that change and new life begin by asking the right questions; Jesus will do the rest.

Clarity about your congregation's part in God's mission. Why are we here? Which of our neighbors needs what we have? What's God already doing in our neighborhood or zip code and how do we hitch on? (Call it "prevenient mission," mission coming to you before you know it's God's.) Get local! What does our congregation offer this part of town that's offered by nobody else? What are our extroverted members already doing in mission, though they may not have claimed it as mission? How can our congregation better support them in their work?

Vision for where God wants you to go from where you are presently most comfortable. What are our strengths? What skills must we acquire in order to be more vibrant participants in God's mission? What do our expenditures tell us about what our congregation most values? What are we doing simply because we've always done it?

Strategies for overcoming introversion by reaching and serving the surrounding community. Narcissism is terminal for a congregation. How much time is our pastor expending caring for our members rather than equipping our members for ministry and mission? How many people do we know who live within a mile of our congregation? Who should we be attempting to reach? What do they need, and how could we serve them by providing it? What is deterring us from being a more welcoming congregation? How can our newest members help us reach more people for whom our congregation would be a blessing?

Tactics for reaching, integrating, and equipping new disciples. It's more fruitful to ask, "Who is not here?" rather than, "How can we get back who we lost?" Ask your newest members how they found your congregation and then ask them to help you find more people like them. What study, growth opportunities are you offering newer, younger Christians? How quickly are you connecting newer members with mission responsibility?

Simplification and acceleration of decision-making and ministry follow-through. How can we spend less time talking and more time doing, less time planning and more execution of our mission? Which standing committees need to become short-term task forces or else end? How should we streamline governance and decision-making so that there's less voting, approving, and control, more risk-taking and experimentation? And how will we hold ourselves accountable to what God assigns us to do? How will we measure progress? Is our church staff pulling in the same direction? Be rigidly determined about mission, flexible about organization and strategy.

Active, resourceful leadership from the pastor. What does this congregation, at this time and place, most need from our pastor? How can we enable our pastor to acquire the needed skills to lead us differently?

To know whether or not these six challenges are yours, the time-honored S.W.O.T. Analysis is a good way to analyze your congregation.

First, focus upon your *Strengths*, your core identity. What gifts are you known for? What are you already doing well? What can be your "on ramp" into the future?

Next, honestly assess your *Weaknesses*. What is your congregation not doing well? Where are your vulnerabilities?

The *Opportunities* that God has given you may surprise you. If the demographics of your neighborhood have changed from the makeup of your congregation, how might that be an opportunity rather than a threat? If you have a large, aging but beautiful building, what makes that a gift rather than an expensive burden?

Threats? A rising age and an absence of children in your congregation are warnings. So is a deteriorating older building, a large debt for the new building, and deep ideological division in the congregation. Being honest about the threats, internal and external, can help build a sense of urgency and focus.

Along with the S.W.O.T. Analysis, get specific information that will help you complete the picture.

1. Tell stories of how your congregation got here. What's your history? Which personalities and events explain where you have come from as a congregation and who you are now?

2. What are your metrics? Trends in attendance and giving. Median age. Income and expenditures. Number of baptisms. Number of people engaged in service to the neighborhood.

3. How do guests perceive your church? Interview your newest members and find out how your church first appeared to them and what attracted them to the congregation. Also ask newest members what they've noticed that ought to be changed.

4. Which programs and strategies have yielded the most fruit in recent months and which appear to be unproductive or to have outlived their usefulness?

Now your congregational leadership will be ready to move toward the essential step—a definition of your mission and purpose.

What Is Your Congregation For?

Because the church is conceived and sustained by powers outside the church (namely, Christ), the church must continually be surprised by and reformed in accordance with its peculiar identity. The single most important question for your congregation to answer right now is, *What aspect of Christ's mission belongs to us?*

Most human organizations get to define their purpose on their own. Easy to come up with a rationale for a Garden Club or a Soccer League, difficult for the Body of Christ.

While it's up to Jesus whether or not to bless your congregation with life, asking and answering, "Why are we here?" is up to you. Neither the UMC nor the GMC can do this purposeful work for your congregation. (How many of you were energized by "Making Disciples for the Transformation of the World"?) Leave or stay UMC, you'll have to wrestle with, *What is our congregation for?*

By asking about purpose, you come to see your congregation as a "means of grace" (Wesley's description of the sacraments), and you acknowledge and embrace your God-given function. Rather than, "Our problem is that we need to keep people from leaving," say, "Our problem is that we haven't defined our purpose clearly enough to keep people loyal to our congregation."

A focused, shared, missional purpose is the most important contributor to congregational thriving. The pastor's talent, vision, or personality? Financial health? Denominational loyalty or antipathy, style of worship and quality of the staff? Ethnicity or politics? None are more determinative of your church's future than your alignment with your purpose as God's people to sign, signal, and witness to the encroachment of God's realm in your neighborhood.

Purpose keeps us going when we don't see visible results and enables us to recover after setbacks. When pastors are unclear about their purpose, the most energetic rush to and fro, fearful that they may neglect the one thing that will give their ministry meaning. The less motivated merely drift, and no church has ever coasted into a vibrant future.

When congregations fail to answer, "What are we here for?" they become distracted, answer to the world's stories that are less than the gospel, major in the minors, and fail to keep the main thing, the main thing. Confused about who they are, they are unable to explain to others why they're here. Who's attracted to an organization that can't name itself?

Your purpose declares not only what you will do but also what you won't. It's okay not to have as your purpose to become a larger church, to be a sort of "boutique church," small, not because you design yourself to be exclusive, but rather because the population you feel called by God to reach is small.

Maybe you will decide that your congregation's mission is to have "beautiful, well-planned, Spirit-filled, unashamedly traditional worship." Go with that, but (1.) Know that you are targeting one demographic group and excluding others, and (2.) Be sure that you have the resources, determination, and quality worship leadership to accomplish that purpose.

The congregation who says, "We want to welcome folks from our neighborhood who are of a different ethnicity," and then fails to secure worship leadership by those of that ethnicity is window-dressing and deluding itself.

Particularly in a crisis, when there is loss, membership decline, and shrinkage of participation in an organization, regrouping around a shared, clear, compelling, and communicable statement of purpose is a matter of life and death. Yet here is our challenge: the church receives rather than devises its purpose. Church consists of those under orders, those to whom the risen Christ has shown up, breathed upon us, and commissioned us to do his work in the world (John 20).

Here's how most Methodist congregations have defined themselves:

> We provide a safe, pleasant, friendly, sometimes inspiring place where you will be with people who share your values, who cherish you and your family's presence and where you'll be given opportunities to worship Christ, serve others in need, and grow in your faith. If you are faithful in your participation in our round of activities, you'll be blessed. We aspire to be an open-minded, welcoming, Christian (but not showy or fanatical), middle-of-the-road fellowship of Christians who promise to welcome you and to care for you when you're in need.

At some point, many found that definition made less sense to our surrounding culture and to many Methodists. Following denominational polity, slapping the Cross-and-Flame logo on our building wasn't enough to keep us together as a church.

"When my congregation split last year, almost disintegrating in a fight over whether or not to wear masks during worship," mused one pastor, "I knew we didn't know why we're here."

Fortunately for your congregation, scripture reiterates the peculiar purposes of God's people:

"But you are a chosen race, a royal priesthood, a holy nation, a people who are God's own possession. You have become this people so that you may speak of the wonderful acts of the one who called you out of darkness into his amazing light. Once you weren't a people, but now you are God's people. Once you hadn't received mercy, but now you have received mercy" (1 Pet 2:9-10).

The church, Christ's body, is the way the risen Christ takes up room in your neighborhood: "God put everything under Christ's feet and made him head of everything in the church, which is his body. His body, the church, is the fullness of Christ, who fills everything in every way" (Eph 1:22-23).

"We are God's accomplishment, created in Christ Jesus to do good things. God planned for these good things to be the way that we live our lives" (Eph 2:10).

A personal favorite: "You will be my people, and I will be your God" (Jer 30:22).

A statement of purpose is a declaration of what aspect of Christ's mission he has assigned to your congregation. What does your church aspire to be known for? What about your congregation is worth sharing? Why should your congregation's constituents fulfill their pledge to support the church with their gifts, attendance, service, and witness?

Some congregational statements of purpose that I have encountered recently:

God's People Pursuing and Signaling God's Kingdom

The Mission Is Fishin'

Grow Believers, Make New Friends, Renew Our
   Neighborhood

Know Jesus and Make Jesus Known to All

Making, Equipping, and Sending More Disciples of
   Jesus Christ

God's Way of Loving Athens

To Grow and to Go with Jesus

Once your congregation comes up with a purpose statement, it must be repeated, reiterated, showcased on the congregation's website, printed on everything. Worship should begin with the leader saying, "Welcome to Trinity where we 'Serve Christ by Serving the Southside of Greenville.'" Church meetings should open with a recitation of the statement. At the end of the meeting, leaders ask themselves, "How has this meeting contributed to the accomplishment of our purpose?"

"Thanks for calling Grace Methodist Church," say those who answer the congregation's phone, "where we 'Love Christ by Loving Our City.' How can I help you?"

Every activity must be accountable to the questions, "Why are you doing this? Is this endeavor getting the response we expected? Is it congruent with our church's mission?"

And just in case your congregation wrestles with purpose and comes up with something resembling, *We're here to be a middle-of-the-road, moderate assemblage of Methodists who think the same and love one another…* If you're the pastor, you're off the hook. It takes little courage or skill to lead that church's purpose. You can stop reading this book now. However, there's little chance that the doors of your congregation will be open for more than a decade.

Fulfilling Our Purpose

From clarity of congregational purpose (What are we for?) we move to a very Wesleyan question: *Now, what are we to do?* Early on, John Wesley asked his Methodists, "What may be the purposes of God in raising up a people called Methodist?" Wesley had the outrageously ambitious notion that he could equip ordinary eighteenth-century English people to be active participants in God's purposes if he taught them holy habits, practices, and disciplines.

Recall Jesus's parable contrasting the house built on sand with the house built on a rock. The "wise builder" not only believes but also takes these "words of mine and puts them into practice." A sure foundation is not so much our set of rock-solid beliefs as it is our putting our beliefs into practice (Matt 7:24-27). Practical divinity.

Thus Wesleyans saw the church as more than a place for believing, for securing your ticket to eternity, or a means of making your life less miserable; church is where we are equipped to live out our vocation in the world. Jesus saves. Jesus calls. Jesus sends.

It's un-Wesleyan to make the gospel mostly about personal fulfillment. The gospel is vocational, Christ's assignment. It's only natural to desire homeostasis, placidity, and rest. Not natural is the dislocation, discombobulation, and pressure that comes with Christ's vocational "Follow me."

While I'm not a fan of much contemporary worship, I am grateful for what initiating an additional, alternative service did for countless churches. All the negotiating, deliberation, organizing, and funding required to start a new worship service caused pastors and congregations to augment their capacities for innovation.

Rather than professional caregivers looking for customers, pastors are lead missionaries recruiting coworkers. As bishop, I saw catatonic congregations awakened through their participation in the UMC Volunteers in Mission. Recruit, organize, and fund a group for a couple of weeks of service in Honduras, you'll energize the congregation. A new generation of North American Christians is uninterested in sending money to the denomination to do mission; they want to be hands-on, face-to-face missionaries.

"Sure, we helped fellow Christians in Haiti," one congregation's VIM leader told me, "but to tell the truth, Haiti did more good for Pleasant Grove than we did for Haiti."

"Want to go on our mission trip to Panama?" a student ministry leader told her students, "invite a friend who isn't a member of a church." Doubled the size of their youth group in one year.

Strategy

Once your congregation gains clarity on your purpose by answering, *What's God calling us to do?* your next question is, *What strategy can get us from where we are to where God wants us to be?*

Strategy must be ruthlessly accountable to your congregational statement of purpose. Simple and achievable. Efficient short-term preparation is more important than cautious long-term planning. Go ahead now. Rather than attempt to devise the perfect plan, commit to being on a journey together, learning from one another, adjusting to changing realities and opportunities, together.

Much of your congregational structure, like your Annual Conference, is designed to serve a world that's gone. You've got too many committees if you've been seduced by the outdated organizational dictums of the *Book of Discipline*. Kill those committees that take too long to make decisions and implement too few initiatives. You need external outreach more than internal stability and order.

A fresh statement of congregational mission will probably require new leadership. In the present moment, it's important for purposeful, missional congregations to have a high percentage of innovators and risk-takers to offset those who chiefly value relationship, consensus, cautious deliberation, and laborious, participatory processes of decision-making. The work that God has assigned your congregation determines who is best to lead.

As you move from purpose to strategy, to leadership and mission engagement, here are some insights that I've gained from hours of conversations with Methodists in recent months:

Money. "Attendance is down but, praise God, giving has kept up." Giving usually lags behind other indicators of congregational health. A few older, loyal, well-formed members keep things going.

Congregations are increasing their cash reserves, squirrelling away resources rather than investing in their future. That "rainy day" for which you are saving is now.

Sometimes, "Our congregation doesn't have financial worries," means that the congregation has a too-modest expectation for its mission.

People give to what's important and whatever they give to becomes more important to them. If you have trouble raising money for a ministry, it could be a sign that this ministry has become irrelevant.

The UMC way of raising money for the general church through denominational apportionments (taxation) has long been unproductive.

Endowments can be dangerous, masking problems in the congregation, tempting members to shirk their stewardship responsibilities.

Participation. There has indeed been a "great resignation" or "great migration." Attendance is down about 30% from three years ago. A similar percentage of clergy say they have considered leaving. Some clergy attrition is due to their delaying their departure until the pandemic ended. For some, unhappiness in ministry before the pandemic was a more important factor in their decision to depart than struggles related to the pandemic or denominational conflict.

Online worship viewing tripled during the pandemic, but few believe that will last or lead to active participation in congregations.

There's been a troubling decline in children's ministry; children's ministry is the most important facilitator of growth in a congregation. Families have been under great stress; church participation is one area that beleaguered families have some discretion over and many are opting out.

Buildings. Amid the "great resignation," many congregations can no longer deny that their buildings are out of scale. Fewer people are interested in making the purpose of the church the upkeep of an aging, dysfunctional building. Some churches have experimented with offering their too-big buildings to service agencies or rental space for cafes and bookstores; most find that it's tough to repurpose church buildings for uses other than church. The income received by a church from renting out space is rarely sufficient to maintain the building. If a church's mission is out of scale with the cost of keeping up the congregation's inherited building, the most practical course of action is to sell the building or vainly try to make the mission the upkeep of the building. The best hope for preservation of the beloved building is for the congregation to give or sell its building to a congregation that has a greater, more biblically mandated mission than the building.

Attendance. Worship attendance continues to be the most important barometer of your congregation's health. Are there patterns of attendance that can be correlated with the style of music or the preacher? Have an honest evaluation of your technology, music, space, and preaching and courageously make the changes that are needed to align your worship with who your congregation aspires to be and who you want to reach.

Engagement. Look at your congregation from the outside in. Have you adequate signage? Parking? Childcare? Is your entrance apparent? (I once served in a church that had twenty-eight exterior doors; only eight were ever unlocked. Newcomers took note.) When my car is serviced, afterwards I get an email: "How likely are you to recommend us to others?" Ask Sunday worship guests, "What do you think we're doing well and what needs improvement?"

No more than 10% of visitors become members. Connection, engagement, affiliation is your first goal for visitors rather than having them actually commit to membership.

Guidance. Get help. Is there a nearby Methodist congregation that appears to be modeling the congregation you'd like to be? Ask for guidance. Study their best practices. Get their recommendation for professional consultants who have been helpful.

Neighborhood. Where do people gather in your neighborhood? Go to them rather than try to get them to come to you. Start a small group gathering at a place other than in your congregation's building.

Website. Is your congregation's website publicly presenting who you aspire to be? If the main feature of your front page is a picture of your building, you're probably looking at your church from the inside out.

Physicality. Online worship is best as a prelude for in-person participation, an accommodation to members who, for reasons of health, mobility, or geography, can't physically be with the congregation, but otherwise it's a bad habit. During the pandemic some of us made the mistake of telling congregations, "Online worship is as good as being here." No, it isn't. In a culture of shrinking in-person life and expanding of virtual life, your congregation has an opportunity again to be a countercultural place for person-to-person, God-to-person encounters.

Location. If you are a small, rural congregation, rejoice! Your church is already well-located, and probably an historic, prominent part of the neighborhood. There's a good chance that a cross section of the community is present when you congregate. Your pastor may be regarded by the community as a leader. You could be one of the best organized groups in town. You're here and you're not going anywhere. Your small scale enables you to do more, faster. Go for it.

Forward, Together

Beset by all sorts of challenges, Matthew bid his church to look back to the first days of the Jesus movement, before they even knew they were a church. The Messiah in whom they had put their hopes had been publicly, humiliatingly tortured to death. Matthew takes them from the traumatic mount of Calvary all the way out to "Galilee, to the mountain where Jesus told them to go" (Matt 28:16-20). What's next?

The risen Christ doesn't offer comforting pastoral care or healing, doctrinal instruction, nor does he speak to them of heaven and the hereafter. Typical of Jesus, he calls and commissions them into the future. Even in their woundedness and loss, they are given assignment, mission, and purpose. Jesus declares that he has "all authority in heaven and on earth. Therefore, go and make disciples of all nations [salvation for all], baptizing them in the name of the Father and of the Son and of the Holy Spirit [giving them authority they could not give themselves], teaching them to obey everything that I've commanded you [even the hard parts about loving your enemies and limitless forgiveness]." Jesus promises [or threatens?], "I myself will be with you every day until the end of this present age [just to make darn sure you obey me]."

The disciples' reaction? "When they saw him, they worshipped him, but some doubted."

Jesus, undeterred by their doubts, "came near and spoke to them." Sometimes when we are grieving, full of doubt, uncertain, and hopeless, it's then that Jesus comes alongside and speaks to us.

Here's my question: *What did they doubt?* Surely the disciples didn't doubt the resurrection. Jesus stood there in front of them. He had been with them on and off for Eastertide's fifty days.

Here's what I think: Some doubted, not the reality of the resurrection, but the possibility of their vocation. Jesus had "all authority." Authority to do what? All authority to call—even those who had forsaken him when the going got rough, his half-hearted, misunderstanding, fearful, failure-to-follow disciples—to "go and make disciples of all nations, baptizing them in the name of the Father and of the Son and of the Holy Spirit, teaching them to obey everything that I've commanded you."

Some doubted the possibility that they still had a role to play in Christ's resurrection future. They questioned if they had a tomorrow beyond today's loss, failure, and grief.

In the face of their doubts, Jesus comes near and promises, "I myself will be with you every day until the end of this present age."

Therein is Methodism's hope. Have we the resources—human, financial, and theological—required to do this work rather than the work we've been doing? Can we get beyond our grief at the loss of Methodism as we have known it? Lord, are you sure we're up to it?

Most of the time our church's challenge is to have faith in Christ. But in the present moment have we half as much faith in ourselves as Christ has in us when he enlisted us to be in motion as the Wesleyan movement? Therefore, in our self-doubt, pray, Lord, "I have faith; help my lack of faith!" (Mark 9:24).

Don't look back. The good old days for Methodism weren't all that good. With the risen Christ, we have more future than past. Here is indubitable hope for your Methodist congregation, hope that even we can courageously step up to the challenges with chutzpa based upon his empowering promise, "I myself will be with you every day until the end of this present age."

Or as John Wesley said with his last breath, "The best of all, God is with us."

METHODIST PASTORS AS MISSION LEADERS

None of this hope-filled, mission-focused-church-in-motion work can be done without the active advocacy, interpretation, and personally committed leadership of the pastor.

There, I've said it.

If only a dedicated group of lay leaders could take upon themselves boldly to define their congregation's purpose, strategize, and stride into the future. Sorry. No congregation outdistances the hopeful leadership of its pastor who sets the ceiling for congregational innovation.

If Jesus Christ had said only "come to me," salvation would be simpler. As soon as Jesus said "Go," along with "Feed," "Love," and "Tell," someone had to step up and take responsibility for helping disciples to be faithful to Christ's summons.

Surely that's why the Acts of the Apostles tells the story the first days of the church by recounting the exploits of the church's leaders like Peter, Philip, Lydia, Mary, and Paul. Once Jesus named us his extroverted "witnesses in Jerusalem, in all Judea and Samaria, and to the end of the earth" (Acts 1:8), the next move was mundane but necessary; appointment of Matthias as replacement apostle (Acts 1:15-26). From the first, no faithful accomplishment of mission without someone stepping up and taking responsibility for getting God's people from where we are to where God wants us to be.

What Are Pastors For?

While the New Testament doesn't dictate how to vet or train church leadership, as early as the Letter to the Ephesians we are told what leaders are for: "He gave some apostles, some prophets, some evangelists, and some pastors and teachers." Pastors are Christ's gifts, not a concoction of the church. Why? "His purpose was to equip God's people for the work of serving and building up the body of Christ until we all reach the unity of faith and knowledge of God's Son" (Eph 4:11-13). Pastors help the church stay together in motion and in mission as the church.

General Conferences' obsession with clergy concerns is clericalism at its worst. We've had divisive, protracted debate over the qualifications and attributes of clergy (Married or celibate? Straight or gay?) without regard for what's reasonable to expect clergy to produce.

Hey, General Conference, while you were debating the proper sexual orientation of clergy, our church shrunk by a third for reasons having nothing to do with the sexual orientation of clergy!

The biblical test for the effectiveness of leaders is not that we've succeeded in keeping everyone calm and comfortable but whether we've equipped "God's people for the work of serving [ministry] and building up the body of Christ." Ordained ministers equip Christ's baptized for their ministry in the world.

The Book of Discipline rightly speaks of the church's leaders as "servants." Trouble is, many clergy have reduced servanthood to servile care-giving for needy personalities in the congregation. Pastors are coordinators of the congregation's care, not the sole givers of care. Besides, sometimes Jesus cares by giving relatively affluent, contented North Americans needs they wouldn't have had, had they not been called by Jesus. We care by helping our congregations get on board with what Jesus is doing, thus giving them better lives than they would have had had not Jesus tapped them for service.

Why pastors? From the ranks of the baptized, God and the church call some to worry about the health of the community of faith as a whole and figure out ways for one generation to give Methodism away to the next. In ordination, fiduciary responsibility is bestowed upon a few to help many have a future with Christ.

In my Introduction to Ordained Leadership class, I tell seminarians, "For most of your Christian life it's been enough for you to tend your garden, to deepen your personal relationship with Christ, and to stay in love with God. Now that you are being called to leadership, you become a *community person*. Your personal concerns must be subordinated to the communal so that you help others encounter Christ and fulfill their baptism."

When Paul speaks "like a crazy person," he crows about his missional accomplishments (2 Cor 11:3-18), bragging that he's been in the slammer multiple times, beaten "more times than I can count" (I would have kept count), stoned, shipwrecked "three times" (!), imperiled by "rivers, robbers, my people, and Gentiles," "in the city, in the desert, on the sea." Fellow pastors note: the worst of Paul's suffering was congregational: "My daily stress because I'm concerned about all the churches."

We may be the first Methodist preachers whom God expects not only to love but also to change the church. As an ordained pastor, discipline your fears and doubts, your need for self-protection, your distaste for conflict, your fascination with denominational politics, and your craving for congregational approval in service of your chief vocation: to serve Jesus Christ by helping him build up, prod, reform, and ignite his churches called Methodist.

Methodist pastors are conditioned to produce order and consistency; now we must learn to lead innovation and improvisation. Thank the Lord you are a preacher; motivating and inspiring is just another Sunday in the pulpit.

You don't need to change everything. Change only that which keeps your congregation from keeping up with a risen, present, peripatetic Christ.

Called to Lead God's People

The rationale for expending your life as a Methodist pastor—submitting yourself to the prodding of the Holy Spirit, subordinating yourself, your marriage, and your family, sometimes even your happiness and safety—is christological. Jesus has put you here. *Vocation.*

Elders, remember the question the bishop asked: *Do you trust that you were called by God to the life and work of an elder?* Nobody can aspire to be clergy. You must be called. Our clergy appointment system, from the first, believed that no congregation can hire a Methodist preacher; preachers are sent.

Before we trust ourselves to be leaders, we must trust God to know what God was doing when God called us so that we can joyfully confess, "I'm here because I was put here. The life I'm living isn't my own. I'm accountable to higher aspirations than attainment of my own happiness or yours. It's not a profession, a pursuit of a personal passion, or an ambition; it's a *vocation*."

Ah, the freedom, when you stand before a divided, contentious congregation that is taking its unhappiness out on you, to know that they don't own you. Their praise or blame cannot validate your ministry. When you fail to accomplish your goals and are fatigued from beating your head against a brick wall, recalling that your vocation is God's idea gives you resilience.

As a young pastor I poured out my frustration to an older, wiser pastor, recounting to him the double offense of my victimization by a dumb District Superintendent and intransigent congregational leadership. My mentor replied, "Write down everything God is calling you to do and then demand that your Superintendent and your lay leaders permit you to be the pastor God has called you to be. If they refuse, quit."

I got his point. I was blaming my own cowardice, laziness, or ineptitude on others. It's so easy, in a hierarchical system, to push responsibility upwards. Once they send us a bishop with good sense, I'll get in gear.

Even if you must leave the UMC, be true to your vocation. The sacrifices you have made (languishing in dull classes on Methodist polity and history, having some bishop tell you where to sleep, tendentious church trustees) should not be disrespected. But before you go, be sure that you are not using the UMC as an alibi for your own leadership limitations or that you are not jumping from a United Methodist frying pan into some Free Methodist fire.

When pastors talk about our congregations, we focus on our problems. But when we speak of our vocation, we tell a story of God's impact upon our lives. Whenever I'm with a clergyperson who is ready to throw in the towel and quit (and there are so many good reasons to do so), I ask, "Tell me about that time when you got the crazy conviction that God was calling someone like you to lead God's people like them."

Whence comes courage to lead? From recollection of and a determination to be true to our calling even when present circumstances tempt us to seek less hazardous work.

Are You the One to Lead Change?

Rather than be a courageous pastoral leader, it's easier to be a busy, unctuous congregational caregiver or a passionate crusader for a cause. In the UMC's present situation, neither caring nor crusading are as important as leading change that gives your congregation a future.

Alas, you've probably received little leadership formation. Your seminary (including the one where I work) is probably unaware that this work even needs to be done much less how to prepare for it.

Remember that Paul said, even though there's one Lord, there are different ministries, all given for the "the common good" (1 Cor 12:4-7). Make an honest assessment of yourself as a leader of congregational change. I greatly respect the pastor who said, after a consultant's review of his congregation, "Bishop, I'm sure that this work needs to be done. But I'm not the guy to do it. You need to get a pastor in here who is better at congregational reformation than I."

Recall the words of Wesley's Covenant Service:

> *Christ has many services to be done.*
> *Some are more easy and honorable,*
>   *others are more difficult and disgraceful.*
> *Some are suitable to our inclinations and interests,*
>   *others are contrary to both.*
> *In some we may please Christ and please ourselves.*
> *But then there are other works where we cannot please Christ*
>   *except by denying ourselves.*

If you encounter constant resistance in attempting to lead change in a congregation, or find that you are spiritually, emotionally drained by this work, ask your bishop to move you to a congregation that wants a future or else find joy in being a hospice chaplain to a dying church.

But before deciding that you can't or don't want to learn how to lead change, recall all those pastoral skills that you have had to acquire. I was clueless about how to ask a congregation for money (in three years of seminary nobody told me I had to raise my salary each year), so I submitted to the indignity of a Conference retreat on financial leadership. After learning a few stewardship best practices, I was able to say at my next appointment, "Financial worries? No problem. I can fix that."

Is it possible that God has given you people in your congregation who love the work you don't? While a pastor can't delegate leadership like preaching, coaching, guiding, referring, vison casting, and oversight, it's possible that God has sent you just the people you need to compensate for skills that God has no intention of giving you.

As bishop, I rarely presided at meetings of my bishop's cabinet—I had trouble sticking with an agenda, didn't like meetings, and knew that my District Superintendents had a deeper knowledge of individual clergy than I. My contribution was to observe my cabinet at work, to ask questions, to make them defend their opinions, thinking about the sum of our decisions and overseeing the process.

I'm a math idiot. Spreadsheets give me hives. Yet as bishop I had responsibility for financial oversight. My "numbers guy" was nearby to respond quickly to the crucial question, "But how much would this cost?"

You'll be unsurprised that my eyes glaze over whenever anybody quotes the *Book of Discipline*. Yet I had a duty to lead without violating the strictures of our connection. My trusty "rules monitor" was always at hand, *Discipline* at her fingertips. However, I said to her, "When we're trying to solve a problem, first tell us what the *Discipline* permits before saying what it prohibits."

Turning Toward the Congregation

As a visiting preacher in a congregation (Sunday attendance, 35), I asked the leaders after service, "What is your greatest challenge?"

The chairperson responded, "The United Methodist Church."

"How so?" I asked.

"When they ordained that gay bishop out west somewhere, that's when lots of us wondered if we could stay Methodist."

A congregation with a median age of about sixty, no children or young families, therefore a church with no more than six or eight years to live, defining their greatest problem as a bishop "out west somewhere"?

Easier to blame the denomination "out there" than to face up to congregational problems right here.

In a hierarchical system it's tempting for clergy to view themselves as passive pawns in an appointive system where they have no control over their destiny. Blame someone up there, out there rather than take responsibility for the shape of your ministry here. That's why I've steadfastly urged you to turn your gaze away from denominational agonies (which you cannot impact) and toward your congregation and its possibilities. "Connectionalism" doesn't mean that the fate of your congregation is determined by the denomination. A bishop can appoint you to a church but can't tell you how to lead that church toward life.

The UMC has had difficulty starting new congregations because we vainly attempted to do this work through the denomination rather than congregations. Methodism had its most dramatic success in planting new churches during the 1950s when churches started churches, though the denomination deserves credit for realizing that to cease planting churches is deadly. Thriving UMC congregations and their pastors, not the Annual Conference, ought to plant churches.

It's your responsibility to do all you can to ensure that your congregation doesn't go down with the inevitable dismantling of the denomination. Leaders face a duty to help the institutions under our care to live (God is whoever invented life and overcame death). Worrying about a way to lead your congregation to vitality is more than anxiety over institutional survival. Call it courage. Resilience overcoming acquiescence.

Sometimes it helps to be an older, seasoned pastor. Whenever a younger pastor says, "My people hyperventilate when I preach about hot button issues," I say, "I entered ministry in a legally racially segregated South Carolina: I find current division and resistance to the gospel unimpressive."

On the other hand, a high percentage of younger, newer clergy may have discovered the UMC during their student days. They thus see the strengths of Wesleyan Christianity and may have less affection for, and less at stake in, previous ways of being Methodist.

When I complained about some aspect of the general UMC, my grandmother-in-law, Bessie Parker (in whose memory is this book), would say, "Dear, don't forget that 'the Methodist church' you have known as a national organization is no more than six decades old. For most of our history the church beyond the Annual Conference was a national meeting every four years with lots of worship and a handful of committees." Somehow, her historical reminder put my pain in perspective.

You may be feeling tired because you are daring to undertake hard work that your predecessors avoided. Maybe Jesus has plopped you in a vocation for which you've got the wrong skill set or disposition. (He loves to pull that stunt.) Some exhaustion may be due to your having been captured by irrelevant, pointless busyness due to a failure to focus and set priorities.

Setting a clear congregational purpose and mission statement and holding yourself accountable to that will help. A priority names that to which we will give attention; what gets our attention gets us. That pastor who is able to say, on the basis of the congregation's mission statement, "It's more important to give this church a future than to keep its present members happy," will find burdens lifted off their conscientious shoulders.

Chapter 2 of the *Discipline* is unhelpful because its ninety pages (!) of rules and regulations (as if our challenge were clergy irresponsibility rather than productivity) fail to focus on what clergy are for.

Poor *BOD*. While you were legislatively churning out more rules, strictures, and prohibitions for clergy, our church nearly died.

The main reason we don't risk or innovate is not laziness but fear, fear of the unknown, fear of failure. By daring to wade into our people's lives of pain, pastors are around lots of letdown. The majority of UMC congregations haven't made a new Christian in the last four years. What UMC pastor is looking for more disappointment? Trouble is, there's no way to work with crucified Jesus and be risk averse.

When your best laid plans flop, say with Job, "The Lord has given; the Lord has taken; bless the Lord's name" (Job 1:21), and try something else. A free and sovereign God is able to bless or not. We ought to hanker for ministry that is so risky that if Christ does not show up and make our work his, it will fail. If we succeed, it's proof that the women running from the tomb on Easter (the first evangelists) were right, "He's risen indeed!"

Some of your weariness and fear are the predictable costs of following a demanding Savior who thinks nothing of sending people like you on outrageous errands. When criticized for his excessive determination to seek and to save the lost, even those whom nobody thought should be saved, including those who didn't want to be saved, Jesus told a story about the good shepherd who relentlessly sought the one lost sheep until tired, then gave up hope for finding and applied for a sabbatical? No. The shepherd sought "until" the sheep is found (Luke 15:4). Good shepherd to your people, keep at it.

The Joy of Being a Conversionist, Sanctificationist Leader

I was never appointed to a growing congregation. But every congregation I served grew while I was pastor. Not all of those churches were happy with me when I arrived, but all were happier with themselves by the time I departed. I enjoy contributing value, receiving satisfaction in leaving a place better than I found it.

Though you may not be naturally inclined to lead transformation, Jesus doesn't care. Sign on with Jesus, you'll have to learn how. Bristol coal miners lapped up John Wesley's deadly dull sermons because Wesley (an implication of his robust confidence in the work of the Holy Spirit) told them that by God's grace they could be better people than they were bred to be. *You* can change. Christ gives "new birth," accepting all sinners who come to him just as they are, but never leaving them as they were. "Growth in grace," sanctification, is God's promise to the baptized. You *can* change. Moreover, Christ—working through converted, moving-on-to-perfection Methodists—is busy changing the world for the better, making this world a foretaste of the one to come when God's will shall be done on earth as in heaven. You can *change*.

And you thought "itinerant" meant moving from one town to another. Sign on with Jesus, be prepared to relocate.

In the ordination service the bishop says that ordinands have been found to possess "the necessary gifts" (talents) and show "evidence of God's grace" for the work of ministry. Grace, Wesleyan grace, is not an affirmative pat on the head as the bishop murmurs, "I love you just the way you are. Promise me you won't change a thing." No. Wesleyan grace is the power of God working in you to give you a life you couldn't give yourself. Grace, Wesleyan grace, is transformative, a sign that God didn't create a world and then retire.

Transforming, redeeming, and reconciling is who Christ is, what Jesus does. "God was reconciling the world to himself through Christ, by not counting people's sins against them. He has trusted us with this message of reconciliation" (2 Cor 5:19). Methodists are bold to believe that Christ continues his reconciling work in us and reconciles the world through us. The Bible loves to tell stories where the only active agent is God. If God doesn't make a way, there's no way. God won't allow us solely to write the story of Methodism on our own.

Because of our christological commitments, just as no Methodist is free to declare, "People can't change," or "That congregation is stuck, and nothing can get it unstuck," so also you can't say, "We will choose which Christians with whom we shall congregate." Any Methodist who walks away from the debate muttering, "I'm tired of arguing about LGBTQ inclusiveness. The conservatives will never change," or "The liberals will never love scripture as much as I," is begging for a lecture in Methodist doctrine.

In conversion, in giving you receive. Any congregation that attempts to be obedient to the Great Commission (Matt 28) will find that extroverting to make disciples will make the congregation better disciples. While converting the world, we are converted, changing the way we do church in order better to be the church Christ means us to be.

What You've Got Going for You

If my summons to lead change sounds daunting, dear Wesleyan Christian leader, take heart. Remember, you've got some things in your favor:

You are capable. In your Methodist ordination, you subordinated your professional advancement, even personal happiness, to leading the mission of the church. If the times call for adaptability, that's good because you've spent your ministry calibrating yourself to congregations you didn't choose, serving places that you would have never picked, had you done the choosing. You fit your leadership to their needs and, in more parishes than not, discovered that you were better suited to lead them than you first thought.

You are sent. That Methodism practices a "sent" rather than a "call" system of clergy utilization is an ever-present reminder that the mission of a congregation is more important than your preferences and limitations. You are sent on the basis of a bishop's assessment of how you can help that congregation hitch on to what God's doing in God's world.

Knowing that you are externally authorized can be empowering. The congregation may push back on your efforts, you may have to talk them into initiatives, but they can't terminate you because they didn't hire you. You were sent. Itineracy is a nice way of demonstrating to your congregation that you are accountable not just to their praise or blame. You are sent. You were not produced by this congregation and its culture, and therefore you may be useful in improving the congregation's culture.

Your goal is not to bed down and stay here your

whole ministry. There's much to be gained from long-term pastoral residency in order to work significant change in a congregation. There's also something to be said for a pastor coming in, leading difficult, controversial work and then moving on as another is sent to build upon the hard-won changes.

"I planted, Apollos watered, but God made it grow," said Paul of one of his congregations (1 Cor 3:8).

Our clergy-sending system, when administered in the interest of mission, can appoint pastors whom congregations might be reluctant to hire, if they were hiring, but are just who's needed to lead into the future. And the system can move pastors out of bad-fit situations without divisive congregational voting and attendant anguish.

The sacrifices you have made to be in ministry compel you to do what you can to ensure that your vocation is honored in your deployment. The Bishop and Cabinet need your help in making wise decisions about clergy placement. Pastors, do your best to articulate your gifts, expectations, and needs. Raise your hand. Show the bishop and District Superintendent what God has equipped you to do, what you have experience doing, and how you thrive. Congregations, present your specific missional leadership needs to appointment makers and insist that they honor your mission in who they send to lead it.

When the appointive system worries chiefly about the happiness and career advancement of clergy under appointment and only secondarily considers the mission leadership needs of the congregation, the system is degraded. Appointment decisions made for any reason, even the most noble, other than finding the very best pastoral leadership for each congregation's mission, are detrimental to congregations and pastors. It's okay to

consider gender and racial equity, past service, seniority (which the UMC doesn't have but acts as if it does),
age, personal aspirations, stands on social issues, or
guaranteed appointment (nothing in the *Discipline*
assures lifetime, unaccountable employment for incompetent clergy). However, when any of these factors takes
precedence over securing the most appropriate pastoral
leadership for a congregation's mission, we've betrayed
the genius of Methodist polity—clergy are for mission
leadership.

You are a preacher. John Wesley's Question 13 of his Large
Minutes defined Methodist preaching as purposeful
and performative: "What is the best general method in
preaching? Answer: 1. To invite. 2. To convince. 3. To
offer Christ. Lastly, To build up, and to do this (in some
measure) in every sermon."

A sermon is therefore a fine occasion to reiterate
and to refurbish the mission of your congregation and
to rally folks around your church's unique purpose.

Leadership changes the world with words, helping
an organization face its problems by telling the truth,
casting a vision beyond where we have become stuck,
and fostering difficult conversations. All of these tasks
are helped by preaching.

Preaching is a primary way that Christ has chosen
to address his people, to call and recall them to join
with him in ministry. A preacher stands up on Sunday,
in the middle of a conversation between God and God's
people, contributes to the conversation through the sermon, and then participates in the continuing coloquy
between God and the congregation for the rest of the
week. Because you are a preacher, you're accustomed to
talking about things that no one wants discussed. You
have a plethora of ways to tell tough truth that maxi-

mize their ability to hear truth they've been avoiding. You've got a captive audience (convened by Jesus) who gather and dare to ask, "Got any word from the Lord?" They asked for it; hand it over.

Subordinating your cherished passions to the biblical text, week-after-week, allowing scripture to say things through you that you would never say had not scripture put you up to it, and presenting a clear, coherent, compelling message offer opportunities that the head honcho of Amazon must envy.

Alas, we've conditioned our people to think that the sermon is about them: they think that a sermon's purpose is to give them advice on how to achieve the purpose they've assigned themselves before meeting Jesus or a time to rally them around an issue that they have decided to be more important than the gospel. No. A sermon is the primary way that Jesus Christ enlists missionaries.

It's not your job to speak definitively to every social issue; your assignment is always to say all that you can, in the best way that you can, to assist Christ in calling to mission every listener he can.

Preaching is a time to read, tell, and recommend the biblical story (Jesus Christ is the whole truth about God), which judges and subsumes all other stories that hold us captive.

When politics, flag, race, economics, education, or sexual orientation are more determinative signifiers than "Christian," it's a sure sign that the master story—God in Christ, the whole truth about God, reconciling the whole world back to God—has taken a back seat to the world's reigning narratives.

Preaching can't do everything. I've never known anybody to change political parties or the way they express their sexuality because of a sermon. Our idols are not so easily overthrown. Jesus is about more important matters than politics, of the left or the right. Politics, patriotism, solidarity with the oppressed, preservation of the nuclear family, protecting the rights of the unborn or the rights of women to choose, and a host of otherwise good commitments are less than the reality of the story about God who is Jesus Christ.

Want to change someone's political point of view? Building upon congregational opportunities for increased relationships will get you further than pulpit-pounding exhortation.

Of course the sermon is an appropriate time to address controversial subjects, particularly if the scripture under consideration calls for it. But again, church is not where we rally around our shared commitments; church is where we are engrafted into and become active members of the Body of Christ in motion.

How sad to see folks bolting from the UMC on the basis of statements that could be written by a conservative political party indignant about statements that could have been written by a liberal political party. The only really good reason for leaving a congregation is christological: "I just don't want to be mixed up with Jesus," rather than "My political positions conflict with what I'm hearing from the pulpit."

"Having had a hellish week—son drinking again, boss in town who's got it in for me—I came this morning seeking comfort and reassurance," she said to me at the door after service.

"I hope my sermon was helpful," I said, nervously.

"Not particularly," she responded. "I came here seeking comfort from Jesus only to have him give me an assignment!" *Methodist.*

You care. In your pastoral care, you have the opportunity
to know your people down deep—their hopes, fears,
sadness, joys, and aspirations. Because you know them
and care for them, you can say tough things to them in
order that they may be equipped and encouraged in their
discipleship.

"You and your new-fangled ideas are going to destroy
this church," said an angry person at the meeting. Knowing that his beloved mother had just died and that his
marriage is on the rocks helped me understand why the
last thing he wants is to lose his church as he has loved
it. His fragility doesn't mean that I cease preaching and
leading, but it does mean that I did so with a better grasp
of the dangerous moves I'm asking him to make.

Then there's the angry person who, in a meeting,
enumerated all the ways that I was giving the church
lousy leadership. He concluded his list of my screw-ups
with, "Still, he's the one who showed up and bailed my
son out of jail so, for all his faults, he's my pastor and
I've got to figure out how to work with him."

When I went out late one rainy night to the city jail,
I thought I was doing pastoral care, working for justice.
Didn't know I was also undergirding my leadership.

You have people's support. Thank God that your people want
you to succeed at being their pastor. Who wants to
admit, "I'm willingly a member of a church whose pastor
is a dolt"? There's a good chance they love their congregation more than you do. In time, you'll leave for another
pastoral appointment; they're staying.

If they believe that you are trying to give their
beloved congregation a future so that there will be a
congregation there for their children, grandchildren,
and the community, their love for their church will be
motivation to help you flourish.

You are not working solo. The Methodist ministry of oversight can be an ally both to you and to the congregation as you undertake the hard work of congregational transformation. Although they don't always function as they should, you're backed up by the collegiality of your Annual Conference and the oversight of your Bishop. As Bishop, I spent an equal amount of time protecting congregations from clergy who didn't know how to love their congregations and supporting clergy whose churches were clueless about how to respond to their pastor. Sad to say, in my eight years as bishop, I had not a single opportunity to defend a pastor from a congregation who complained, "Our pastor is so forcefully leading us forward that we can't keep up. Send us a less insistent leader."

    Bad things happen when clergy conceive of themselves as free agents, Lone Rangers who are unaccountable to anyone but the laity. The checks and balances offered by Methodist polity and the ministry of clergy oversight can reassure Methodist laity that their pastors will be accountable to clergy colleagues. (Making it all the more sad when some say they are leaving the UMC because a few clergy and bishops have not been held accountable to the standards of our connection.)

You have a conference. You can be prodded and inspired in your work by the innovative, experimental work of your Annual Conference. Admit it: For any of the Conference's faults, most of the training and encouragement for clergy—to start new congregations, to turn around declining churches, to engage in camp and campus ministry in order to make new generations of Methodists, to provide safe sanctuaries for children and youth—has come from workshops, consultations, coaching, and pleading from agents of the Annual Conference.

You have the Discipline. *The Book of Discipline*, for all its faults, gives your congregation the structure and form it needs to do this work. You don't have to reinvent the organizational wheel. Say what you will about the *BOD*'s dated rigidity, to tell the truth, the *Discipline* gives more flexibility, adaptability, and opportunity for creativity than most congregations have had the courage to use.

Be skeptical of the pastor who says, "I would, but the *Discipline* won't let me." The *BOD* can be either an alibi for avoiding risky work or a prod to do difficult, necessary organizational renovation.

You have a congregation. Thank the Lord that your responsibility is for the transformation of a congregation, or the couple of congregations on your charge, not for the whole denomination. You stand a better chance of convincing ten leaders who love their congregation than a Bishop has of convincing six hundred in the Annual Conference. The small scale of most Methodist churches is in your favor. As Bishop, when I was discouraged by my inability to mobilize my Annual Conference, I found that a weekend spent in a thriving local church lifted me out of the dumps. The more you focus upon a specific congregation, the less you fret over the fate of a whole connection, the happier you'll be.

You are a learner. It would be incredibly ungrateful of you not to admit that you got your theological education from schools that were funded by the Ministerial Education Fund, the most generous seminary support program of any denomination. You have been adopted into an ecclesial tradition that has, from the first, valued a learned ministry, knowing that pastors are made, not born, through lifelong reading, thinking, and growth in grace. That you are reading this book is a sign that you have been well-formed in how to read your way out of whatever fix Christ and his church have put you in. Congratulations.

You can get help. For most of us, leadership of the congregation will require the courage to step outside of our comfort zone (doing work that we know how to do, work that worked for us in the past) in order to refit ourselves for new challenges. Lots of help is available. In research for this book I listened to hundreds of podcasts from church consultants, pastors, and church researchers. There is more available knowledge and experienced insight for leading your congregation than in the entire history of our church.

Had I the time and you the patience, I'd show that you are fitting yourself to lead a new UMC (or are so discontent that you are thinking about leaving the UMC) because you have been so well-formed by the UMC. Lots of Christian leaders could care less about who their church is overlooking and are as happy as pigs in mud with their congregations in decline.

Not you. In your discontent and restlessness, in your determination to get your flock in gear with Jesus, you do Father John proud.

Chapter 7

BEST PRACTICES OF TRANSFORMATIVE METHODIST LEADERS

After listening to hundreds of American Methodists, interviewing leaders in dozens of congregations, I've found some best practices for those who want a Methodist future.

- Leaders go first. The leader's alignment with the congregation's statement of purpose precedes the congregation's. Today's pastors are more scrutinized and criticized because they are more needed. (Who needs leadership when everyone is already walking in the same direction?)

  Leaders go first in modeling risk, being willing to fail, regroup, and start over. The leader goes first in reflection, realization, and repentance, publicly owning past failures, forgiving them, and committing to new directions. Leaders go first in building new relationships with people from different backgrounds, modeling humble listening and learning, and finding ways to get beyond the confines of the congregation and out into the community.

  As the pastoral leader you probably have the most to lose in the transition from old to new Methodism.

You also have the most to learn in your transition from the pastor you thought you might be to the one who's required now. Be willing not only to fail but also to be surprised that God is actively with you even when you aren't sure how things will turn out.

• Congregations tend to reward their pastor for not rocking the boat and punish for attempting to lead change. A leader who is convinced of the righteousness of this work must be prepared for times of discomfort, loneliness, and opposition. No resistance is usually a sign of no movement in mission. If some people take their money and leave, their departure could be a sign that you are at last making headway.

• Congregations love placidity. A transformative leader's job is to keep applying pressure, to persist in asking uncomfortable questions, and to raise the heat, lowering the thermostat just before things boil over. But please note: most of us paternalistic/maternalistic pastors overestimate a congregation's inability to withstand pain. When they whine "please stop making us uncomfortable" say, "I'm not the one who called you to discipleship. Take it up with the Lord!"

  Leaders who veer too far from a congregation's core culture and identity look back and find they have no one to lead. What in your congregation's history shows that they already know how to do the work that must be undertaken now?

  "I'm sure we can find a way to muddle through a debate about same-sex marriage," said the Lay Leader. "Remember when we had that big fight over whether or not to relocate? We made it through that without losing much blood. This church knows how to have a knock-down-drag-out argument followed by kissing and making up."

- If there are those who need to leave in order to stay alive as Christians, bid them farewell but not without giving your best shot to talk them out of leaving. Sometimes they are the people whose discontent, high standards, and expectations are needed to get the congregation unstuck. Plead, "Don't leave us. I need you to keep questioning me, to hold me accountable, to notice things I overlook."

    If your congregation says upfront, "Our purpose is the care and comfort of the few people who are here as a legacy from the hard work of previous generations of pastors," you'll hear a sigh of relief from the Bishop. Pastors whose skills are limited to unctuous, empathetic caregiving are a dime a dozen. Finding well-equipped, courageous pastoral leaders is hard work that many bishops and cabinets are looking for an excuse to avoid. Let the bishop send a pastor to them who is a caretaker (who will eventually be an undertaker) as you are sent to a congregation who wants to go places with Jesus.

- Stay physically, intellectually, spiritually fit for ministry. Sabbaticals, workouts at the gym, longer prayer time, deeper dives into scripture, diet—these practices protect the gifts God has given you. Budget your time so that you are able to fulfill your vocation to marriage and family (if God has given you those vocations) so that they will benefit from, rather than be in competition with, your vocation to ministry. Cultivate friendships; Jesus begins his mission by putting people in a group and then sending them out two by two (Luke 10:1). Lone Rangers don't last long as pastoral leaders.

- Free your congregation from captivity to my generation and its mores. Check out the median age of the UMC or the GMC and you'll know why it's imperative to spend more time with younger people and newer members of the congregation. If the choice is between visiting homebound members (many people would be better at that than the pastor) or hanging out with a new generation of potential Methodists at the coffee shop or bar, your congregation's statement of mission will tell you what to do.

- Particularly after the isolation and disconnection of the pandemic, this is not the season for quiet reflection or keeping silence. It's time for communication, connection, interaction, and engagement. Overcommunication is impossible during a crisis. Look for opportunities to talk, to listen, to argue, and to dream with people within and outside of the congregation, for openings to bring up, reflect upon, and reiterate the congregational statement of purpose. Rather than low-energy chat, "How are you and the family?" better to ask, "Got any ideas about how we can better live up to our aspiration to be the People of God in mission?"

  Have you had a face-to-face conversation with opponents of your leadership? It's natural not to want to hang out with those who push back. Some critics just want to be heard; others may speak truth that no one cares enough about you or the fate of the church to say. Try not to be defensive and argumentative. Be an appreciative, charitable listener: "Can you say more?" "Got ideas about how I can be more effective?"

  Depressed, concerned about your congregation? Get out and visit folks at home, school, or where they work. I guarantee that the Lord will insinuate himself into those conversations and you'll come back refreshed for leadership.

  The greater the crisis, the more fierce your opposition, the greater the need for talk, talk, talk. Don't believe me? Note how the bishops' relative silence has only exacerbated the threat of UMC division.

An active member of your congregation stops attending or giving? Could be a cry for conversation. No person should withdraw without being asked, "Can we talk?"

- Emphasize not congregational weaknesses but rather strengths, resources, and the help at hand. Begin with the faithful few who want a future. Be surprised by who God sends you to help.

- In the pandemic, pastors who wanted to stay in the game led their churches in a rapid embrace of digital media technology, making the past couple of years the century's most active, creative period of church innovation.

  Diverse digital platforms have enabled expansion of congregational boundaries. We have learned what technology is good for (increasing time to get things done, shrinking geographic distance) but also what it can't do well (provide a sense of community and deep, formative interaction). Online platforms level the playing field for small churches; even the smallest congregations can have a great web page, inexpensively expanding their public face, enabling constant contact, and offering convenient meetings. But technological media tends to be a better front door than a continuing, formative space. There's no substitute for face-to-face, sacramental, bodily contact.

  "I take a moment in the service to speak directly to our online viewers," said one pastor. "Telling them, 'We want to know you. Text me!' My email address and phone number float across the screen. Our goal is to make viewers into active participants."

- Church staff must be aligned with your congregation's mission. Growing congregations have a smaller proportion of paid staff than congregations in decline. Staff can coach, train, oversee, and convene congregation members for the

fulfillment of the congregational mission, but they can also
rob the baptized of their baptismally bestowed vocations.

It's easier to raise money to pay staff than to recruit
and empower congregational leadership. (Oops; almost
said "volunteer leadership." Christ gave none of us the
opportunity to volunteer.) Declining churches try to
solve problems by adding staff. A large staff boosts the
pastor's self-image and relieves the pastor of onerous
responsibilities, but staff also can distract the pastor
from equipping the saints, recruiting leaders, and paring
programs and ministries that no longer contribute to the
congregation's purpose.

Need more money for mission? Get more members
into day-to-day mission; the money will come.

• Expect trouble. No leadership occurs, no organization
thrives or survives, nobody follows Jesus Christ free of
conflict. Few pastors like conflict; surely there must be
some way to follow Jesus without getting hurt.

No. Martin Luther King's "Letter from Birmingham
Jail" told his presumed white clergy allies that the
powerful rarely give the powerless their due without a
fight. Conflict may be a sign that the voiceless are at last
being heard or that we are finally doing work we have
avoided for decades.

You'll know you are successfully leading change
when the heat is turned up ("conflict" is from the Latin,
confligere, "to light a fire"). Polite Methodists push back
only when pushed. Truth is always contestable; Jesus is
notoriously willing (sometimes, eager) to foment conflict
and to push his followers into the middle of it.

The bishops' desire for "gracious exit" and "charitable
listening" to those who would dismantle the church
the bishops are supposed to defend could be a cover for

some bishops' reticence to engage in difficult, conflicted conversations.

The enemies of transformative leaders are contentment, harmony, and self-satisfaction. A happy congregation is often one that has given up too soon. Maybe the only gift of the pandemic was to cause contented pastors to become innovators, whether we wanted to or not.

Conflict can be an opportunity to ask, "Why are we here?" "What is it that we most love about this congregation?" "Are the things we are fighting over relevant to and necessary for the accomplishment of our mission?" "Are we making too much of our differences and too little of our commonalities?" "Is this crisis a problem to be resolved by taking a vote and making a decision or is this probably destined to be an ongoing, chronic debate that no vote will stifle?"

BTW: The predominate reason given by clergy for leaving the UMC for the GMC is fatigue over conflict about sexuality issues. They will find that the GMC is no haven from conflict (except from disagreement over one social issue).

Good conflict is the result of having necessary arguments about the urgency of the congregation's mission and how to accomplish it. Bad conflict is fighting over ideological differences (which Wesley called "nonessentials" or "opinions"). It's hard to resolve ideological conflict and anyway, why must such conflict be resolved in order to further the mission of Jesus Christ? Having a clear, agreed upon statement of purpose and mission is your friend in managing divergence.

How much conflict is too much? Enough to be sure people have been heard, not enough to destroy the congregation. Dissident voices need to be heard but then responded to with, "Thanks for your feedback," or "It appears we have a disagreement." If all else fails, "We're not going to do what you want us to do; I hope that won't detract from your commitment to the mission of the congregation."

John 13:35 does not have Jesus say, "see how democratically they split up from one another." Intrachurch conflict has never attracted people to a congregation. Conflict is most dangerous when unmanaged or avoided. Not acknowledging or suppressing differences causes conflict to fester as dissident voices feel they've been squelched.

Pastors name the elephant in the room, set the table, offer space and time for conversation, establish and enforce boundaries and ground rules for debate. Pastors may have to forego their natural inclination to be the accepting, affirming, givers of care and adopt a more "parental" posture, refereeing among combatants, ensuring that dissident voices are heard without suppressing anyone's witness, listening for nuances and complexities in a debate that's simplistically presented as either "traditional" or "progressive," policing bullies, teaching people how to fight like Christians in the church.

Externalize and depersonalize conflict. It's not about you; it's a discussion about how we should participate with Christ in his mission.

Do some of the combatants need to leave the conversation? That drastic step occurs only after prayerful pastoral intervention and deliberation. If you do what's required, you'll probably lose some members who are frustrated by their lack of power to control the congregation. Of course, they'll claim to be leaving because of "biblical authority" or "Christian values," but the main reason will be that they can't get their way.

However, you will keep some people who would have departed a dying church and you may attract some new members who are grateful for a church that's clear about its mission.

It's too easy for pastors to count those few who walk out in a huff but fail to note the many who have given up on their church and have just drifted away. Pay attention to the new people for whom Methodism is the gift they're grateful to receive.

- Voting, rather than resolving a conflict, produces winners and losers, makes conflict worse as the majority forces its will on the minority. I saw a congregation demoralized because the Reconciling Movement insisted that the congregation take a vote in order to join them. The vote failed to pass by a margin of less than five percent. Those who voted against were labeled homophobic, and the vast majority were angry.

It's downright un-Methodist to respond to agitation to separate from the UMC with, "Let's take a vote!" Nobody knows what life apart from the UMC will look like. A vote to leave doesn't address the most pressing problems of a declining church, cannot guarantee the end of Christian disagreements about LGBTQ+ inclusion, and unleashes all sorts of unhealthy, distracting dynamics within a congregation. (Would that we had not taken a vote at the end of the St. Louis General Conference!) It's horrible that, through voting, a majority of a congregation can force out of their church the loyal minority who want to stay UMC.

Voting pushes people into simplistic either/or positions, denying the diversity and complexity of an argument. When the conflict within a congregation appears to be two-sided ("traditionalists" vs. "progressives") sometimes a leader's strategy is to move participants from a fight between Option A or Option B to a more charitable, supple Option C. Not UMC or GMC but how about a new, more missional and therefore more faithful MC?

Rather than "let's take a vote," the wise pastor asks questions like, "What would it take for you to continue in fellowship with this congregation?" Or "Could we cease attempting to solidify this congregation's stand on same-sex unions (which seems impossible at present) and instead name what's required to stay together in this church?" Or "Could we allow same-sex unions to be celebrated by promising that we will evaluate the experiment a year from now and see if we want to continue?" Or "We want to be an open, inclusive congregation, but for the time being, while we won't perform same-sex unions, we will stay in prayer and conversation about the matter, and we will keep open to the leading of the Holy Spirit."

- Empathy—the ability to feel another's pain—is a fine pastoral leadership virtue but can also be a cover for cowardice—easier to sympathize with people in their pain than to hold them accountable for living out their vocation as disciples, even in their pain. Overly empathetic pastors can become overwhelmed by people's pain. Protective paternalism of sensitive, fearful, needy people becomes the goal of their ministry rather than mission leadership. Mute empathy is always more gratefully received than truth-telling by everyone. Except Jesus.

When I asked a pastor why he didn't engage his congregation in conversation about their future, he replied, "If I told my congregation the truth that they are a dying church, it would kill them." Ironic, huh?

When members plead, "If we change this, we could hurt the feelings of some of our most devoted members," it's an indication that some have learned, "If we play to our pastor's need to see himself as loving, caring, and empathetic, he'll stop hurting us by telling the truth."

Empathy must be disciplined with resolve. The congregational mission enables us to say, as we are leading difficult, potentially conflicted change, "I'd like to get through this without causing discomfort and loss, but we probably can't." Take up the cross.

- There's no way to work with the risen Christ without being caught in the middle of contentious, stress-filled conversations between Christ and his people.

You probably look back fondly on your first days of ministry in your first dear, difficult congregation because, when you were young, clueless, and nervous, the mission compelled you to be creative and courageous. Stress is another name for God-induced pressure that produces energy that leads to creativity. When I've got a tough biblical text to preach, I'm stressed into producing a livelier sermon.

Say, "I want to please everyone and receive love and gratitude from all my parishioners," you'll need a healthy dose of stomach medicine.

Stress can be a sign that we're the wrong person at this place and time for this job, an invitation to ask, "Is this really the sort of ministry I'm willing to do?" Respect those who—on basis of an assessment of their gifts and the contentiousness of their congregations in the present—decide that they don't want to be pastors.

The trick is not to waste time stressing out on matters over which we have little control or impact and to learn to enjoy the peculiar stress induced in sinners like us by Jesus's "Follow me."

Best Practices for Pastoral Leaders of Change

Here's a grab bag of a few of my pastoral leadership learnings over the years:

- Celebrate small steps. The Exodus from enslavement began with one step.

- Identify and empower the few who get things done. The traditional leaders you inherited likely have too much at stake in preserving the status quo that was produced by them. Don't tackle too many things at once; stick with what is essential and possible. Play the short game. Give the congregation a few quick wins.

- You don't have to bring everyone on board before you move forward. Consensus on risky, difficult initiatives is too much to ask. Give intransigent individuals the dignity of not being forced to approve of and participate in every ministry of the church. Waiting until everyone is on board disempowers those who are ready to take risks; risk takers are in short supply. No member or group should be given veto power over change.

- Count the yes votes.

- Keep at it! Change, no matter how needed, requires dogged persistence. Don't give up too soon. We Methodists who cherish a tradition of pastoral itinerancy may need to admit that many congregations need longer pastorates to do the work of change.

- Be careful standing in the middle of the road; that's where the dead animals are. By attempting to stand in the middle of an argument, pastors imply that they have discovered superior high ground that has been overlooked by the combatants. Both sides suspect that the middle-minded pastor is without principle, "lukewarm and neither hot nor cold" (Rev 3:16). Better than some placid middle, stand with Christ on a ground that is often conflicted and cruciform. In Methodism, the "golden mean" can be an excuse for leaden mediocrity.

On the other hand (ambivalence, a Methodist theological virtue!), the leader is sometimes accused of standing in the middle of an argument when it's more accurate to say that the leader stands in solidarity with the institution's health and survival. That's not the middle; it's that place of quiet courage. "My calling is to ensure that this dispute does not end our togetherness."

- We can say no to demands upon our time and attention out of a conviction that Jesus told the truth: God, "is still working, and I am working too" (John 5:17).

- You need not be good at both management and leadership, but you must find someone who can make up for your shortcomings. Leaders are big-picture people; managers offer hands-on oversight. Managers ask, "Where?" and leaders ask, "Why?"

  Managers do the time-consuming, unglamorous work required to get things done; leaders worry about doing the right things. When laity complain about their pastor's leadership, they often complain about deficiencies in management: long, agenda-less meetings, missed appointments, taking too long to respond to emails, etc. These are easy to fix.

  Pastors must be efficient, skilled managers if their leadership is to have impact, *and* pastors must be risk-taking, visionary leaders if their management is to be more than rearranging deck chairs on the *Titanic*.

- Take heart. Leadership books tend to stress the talents, personality, and intelligence necessary to be the perfect leader. While Christians are not excused from the self-discipline and the competencies required for effective leadership, you became a leader not because of your superior gifts but on the basis of Christ's "Follow me."

- Count and measure. Counting asks, "How many did we get?" Measuring asks, "How far have we come?" Stop comparing your current attendance with pre-pandemic attendance. Rather than simply measure attendance and giving, ask, *Who have we met? How will we know when we have opened our door wider? How much better aligned are we with our congregation's purpose?*

  No purpose, no goals; no goals, no measurement; no measurement, no wins. Make goals a stretch, but also realistically reachable. You're not looking for any more failures; you need multiple small victories. Children's ministry contributes more to congregational growth and vitality than student/youth ministry.

  You count only what's important and whatever you count becomes important. I may tell you I'm on a diet but until I get on the bathroom scales and notice the numbers, I'm not on a diet.

- Help the church to craft a new story. Rather than the tired, nostalgic narrative of how we used to be something and now we're next to nothing, tell a new story of perseverance, loyalty, and the wonder of folk caught up in the grand pageant of Christ's salvation. As a preacher, you probably have gifts for storytelling. Dignify the vocation of ordinary Christians by pointing to, cheering on, and announcing their victories.

- Don't look back. It is the calling of the church not to
  allow external factors to determine us, to refuse to let our
  historical, geographical, cultural context set the boundaries
  of what is possible for the congregation. Don't look back.

Don't Look Back

In the middle of one of his best letters, written to a congregation in the middle of (what else?) congregational debate, Paul
takes a swipe at some unnamed opponents, warning, "Watch out
for the 'dogs'" (Phil 3:2). (Need I advise you not to call people
"dogs" during church fights?) We assume Paul's canine adversar-
ies were those who "insist on circumcision" (3:2). Give thanks
that the church solved that one without division. If these Jews
could dispense with the biblical requirement for male circumcision (even after Paul had called some of them "dogs"), why can't
today's Methodists resolve matters that have scant scriptural interest? But that's a sermon for another Sunday.

Paul briefly brags of his stellar Jewish credentials—
"circumcised on the eighth day," lifelong member of "the people
of Israel and the tribe of Benjamin," "Hebrew of the Hebrews,"
and "blameless," though there was that unfortunate business
when "I harassed the church" (Phil 3:5-6).

Then Paul catalogues the misery he has suffered because of his
vocation. Of his losses Paul says, "I wrote them off as a loss for
the sake of Christ" (Phil 3:7), nothing more than "sewer trash"
(3:8) when compared with the opportunity to know "Christ, the
power of his resurrection, and the participation in his sufferings"
(3:10). (The hassles and suffering of church leadership draw one
closer to Christ?)

Paul doesn't claim that he has "already reached this goal or have already been perfected [good Wesleyan word], but I pursue it, so that I may grab hold of it because Christ grabbed hold of me for just this purpose" (3:12). Nice definition of discipleship. A Christian is not first of all someone who subscribes to a set of orthodox doctrines or has achieved the right posture on all social and ethical issues. A Christian is anybody "grabbed hold of" for Christ and his purposes.

Then Paul says something that gave me the title for this book. "But I do this one thing: I forget about the things behind me and reach out for the things ahead of me" (3:13), in pursuit "of God's upward call in Christ Jesus" (3:14). Not looking back, Paul looks forward because that's where he will most likely see a resurrected, living Christ.

Don't look back to the general church or denominations old or new to guide you; look to Christ. Dare to have as much faith in the future of your congregation as Christ has in you. Risk believing that Christ has a role for you to play in his grand retake of his world, to be his agents, his ambassadors who look forward to that day when his will shall be done on earth as in heaven.

Look Forward in Hope

Christian hope is based not upon faith in well-applied leadership techniques or in the congeniality of Methodists. Our hope is that this story is true:

The first Easter morning, when things looked really dark for the Jesus movement, "Mary Magdalene and the other Mary came to look at the tomb" of crucified Jesus. (Where were the male disciples? That's another story.) A "great earthquake" shook them. An impudent angel sat astride the stone that had once shut the tomb's door. The soldiers guarding the tomb were as good as dead. The angel told them not to look back: "Don't be afraid. I know that you are looking for Jesus who was crucified. He isn't here, because he's been raised from the dead, just as he said. Come, see the place where they laid him. Now hurry, go and tell his disciples, 'He's been raised from the dead. He's going on ahead of you to Galilee. You will see him there'" (Matt 28:1-7).

Sorry. Just missed him. The One who had a tendency to walk ahead on the road does so again. First day of his resurrected life, where's Christ? He goes to Galilee. One might have thought he would have gone back to the palace to confront the powerful. "Pilate, you made a big mistake. It's payback time."

No, the risen Christ goes forward to Galilee where his movement began, to Galilee, notorious Gentile hangout, the outback from which his first disciples were hewn.

Christ doesn't wait for us to come to him; he comes to us, coming all the way out to Galilee. Most Methodist congregations are not large, powerful, and impressive; from the first the genius of Methodism was to plant communities of faith in places other churches left behind. Places like your neighborhood, Galilee.

As the angel told the women, that's where we'll see Christ, the place where he chooses to look for us, meeting us there before we know how to meet him. That's Methodist hope.

Chapter 8

WITH JESUS
IN THE STORM

Easter week, after tornadoes tore through Alabama, destroying a dozen Methodist churches and parsonages, I stood in the rubble of a rural church and proclaimed, "We will rebuild your beloved church. The Conference stands with you. Thank the Lord you paid up your insurance!"

Afterward, just before departing in my bishopmobile, the pastor said, "Bishop, wish you hadn't gone on and on about 'building back.'"

"What?"

"There's a congregation of Black United Methodists a mile down the road. We've had a few events together. Their pastor and I have prayed about uniting our two little churches, with us as co-pastors. But the people smacked down every effort to merge.

"Now, I'm not saying that God was behind that tornado. I'm just saying that if God wanted us to be more faithful, and if God got tired of waiting for us to do the right thing, and if God decided it was time to step in and push us to do something we didn't have the guts to do, well…"

A theology of divine agency too rare in our connection.

127

The UMC is in a storm of dismantling. I'm not saying that God tired of waiting for us to reform ourselves and get back in step with Wesleyan missionary Christianity. I'm just saying…

While I'm an agnostic on whether or not God sends ill wind to teach a lesson, I'm a firm believer that a creative, redemptive God can use even destructive storms to stir us up and energize us for our true vocation.

Only a week after my visit to that devastated rural church, I stood in the gym of a suburban church that had been converted into a disaster relief center. Earlier, I had visited the congregation at the behest of the pastor. He had reported numerous ongoing disputes: broke budget, the new parking lot, the pastor's bomb of a sermon on the Third Sunday of Lent, somebody directing the praise band who had fired the lead guitarist. Usual fare for a fragmented, unhappy church.

After a contentious meeting with the congregational leadership, I told the pastor, "I'll talk to the Cabinet about possibilities for getting you out of here this June. Can you hang on until then?"

But now, after the tornadoes, I saw a busy pastor orchestrating the feverish activity of disaster relief.

"Got a doublewide full of disposable diapers to unload, Bishop, so I don't have time for much talk," the pastor explained. "I've never been more proud of this congregation. Two-thirds of them are involved in our relief work. And we've attracted about forty volunteers from outside our church since they're so grateful for what we're doing."

"When you've got time," I said, "let's talk about your move that we discussed when I was last here."

"Are you crazy? I ain't moving nowhere! God has made this church what we should have been all along. When those tornadoes blew through town, a bunch of bad wind became the Holy Spirit. *Maranatha*!

"Got to get back to offloading diapers."

Methodism is buffeted by a storm. A destructive, death-dealing gale? Or could it be a fresh infusion of Holy *Pneuma*? Will we just batten down the hatches and ride out the tempest, picking up debris afterwards and attempting to reconstruct the church we had? Or will a redemptive God use our current disruption to make us the church we should be? How typical of God to push us toward a future without our knowing for sure where we're headed.

Throughout this book, my conviction has been that our fragmentation distracts Methodists from deeper, long-term issues that are more determinative of our future than the present turbulence. I've urged UMC pastors and congregations not to be preoccupied with denominational disorder. Take a hopeful look at your congregation, refocus upon the mission that God entrusts to your church, and flip Wesley's "the world is my parish" to "my parish is this neighborhood."

But it would be dishonest to ignore our stormy separations. Before we end, let's ask what Methodists need to learn from our fragmentation.

Dividing

For the first time in a century, a number of elders have decided that God has not enabled them to keep their ordination vows to

Be loyal to The United Methodist Church,
    accepting its order, liturgy, doctrine, and discipline,
      defending it against all doctrines contrary to God's Holy Word,

and accepting the authority of those who are appointed
to supervise your ministry.

("The Order for the Ordination of Elders" *The United
Methodist Book of Worship*)

These clergy are leading some laity to believe that God didn't
give them the grace to keep their church membership promise:

As members of Christ's universal church,
will you be loyal to the United Methodist Church,
and do all in your power to strengthen its ministries....
by your prayers, your presence, your gifts, your service and your
witness?

("Baptismal Covenant I," *The United Methodist Hymnal*)

No Methodist, clergy or lay, would break their promises without strong convictions. I reiterate: there are legitimate criticisms
of The United Methodist Church, its organizational culture,
confused theologies, and leadership mistakes. If you don't have a
list of what's wrong with the UMC, I'll loan you mine. I've not
dodged UMC quandaries. And yet, few of those problems can be
solved by the *Book of Discipline* of the UMC, nor by separating
from the UMC. I understand the outrage when the Council of
Bishops doesn't discipline its own when they violate church law. I
agree that when the COB failed to convene General Conference,
they looked weak and irrelevant.

The COB's divisions and inability to lead in the present moment is a mirror of the divisions within your Annual Conference,
maybe even your own congregation. Let the failed mechanisms of
the general church be a warning, but please, *please don't offer them
as a legitimate reason to divide the UMC.*

Most people in your congregation have never heard of the
Council of Bishops, can't name their bishop, and have never run

across a real, live member of General Conference. In their uncon-cern for the church beyond their congregation, they have things in proper perspective.

We bishops have some repenting to do. If the major function of bishops is acquiring mission-minded pastors for each congre-gation, who bears responsibility for our crisis of congregational leadership? There's no such thing as "guaranteed appointment" in the UMC. No disciplinary sanction forces a bishop to appoint an incompetent pastor to an unsuspecting church. There is no seniority in clergy appointment even though most Cabinets act as if there were. Anytime we bishops veer from the missional leader-ship criterion for clergy placement, we risk losing the faith the laity put in us to administer the church for the good of their con-gregation's mission.

"I would love to be able to defend staying UMC," a lay leader told me, "but two pastors in a row have been appointed here for reasons other than being a good fit for our leadership needs. We even cut our pastor's salary because somebody said that would get our congregation off the list of plums for soon-to-be retired pastors." If his two-thousand-member congregation leaves the UMC, the Conference will lose the third largest contribution to the Conference budget including the biggest donation to the Episcopacy Fund.

The 2012 General Conference in Tampa was a watershed. Af-ter hard work and prayerful negotiation, the Council of Bishops led and the General Conference miraculously agreed to a new plan of operation, a simplified form of church governance with stress on mission and adaptive contextualization. The Judicial Council prohibited the plan.

Now, we must turn from the general church and denominational legislative mess and back to the Annual Conference and the local congregations of the Annual Conference. The core of the Methodist movement—predating the creation of General Conference—is a connection of elders in conference with one another, deployed in local churches for word, sacrament, and order, by appointing bishops.

Our hierarchical, unimaginative administration of UMC polity is more a commentary on our lack of courage and creativity than on strictures of the *Book of Discipline*. Some UMC Conferences are experimenting with having a congregation declare to the Appointive Cabinet intent to be "traditional" or "progressive." (In a way, this is fairly standard; competent Cabinets have always asked congregations to define their mission for purposes of clergy appointment.) Then the bishop and cabinet attempts to honor the congregation's statement of its identity. Thereby, the Conference is trying to retain those who might otherwise leave. (Though I hope any congregation that so defines itself would be questioned about its priorities for mission. The self-applied label is an indication that the congregation is probably thinking internally—"Who are we?"—rather than externally—"What is Christ up to in our neighborhood?")

We must experiment, trying new forms of clergy appointment and congregational organization. The purpose of the connection is not to foster boring, top-down uniformity and beige mediocrity but to strengthen the local congregation in mission, strong congregations encouraging weaker ones, working together in Wesleyan mission.

Why can't clergy exercise discretion in performing same-sex unions where the law allows? If California Methodists figure out a way to stem their rapid decline through some creative act of Christian mission and outreach, could North Carolina Methodists applaud and learn from them? Why not let congregations decide how and who they will reach in their neighborhoods?

Ordination—selecting, vetting, and receiving clergy—has historically been the prerogative of Annual Conferences. Once General Conference insinuated itself into ordination with its lists of requirements, years of hoops to jump through, papers to write, and sexual practices to be debated, well... Can't we again trust the Annual Conference to handle its God-given mission to select, train, and ordain the clergy who serve in the Conference?

Where would we be if some Methodist Conferences and bishops had not defied General Conference legislation and pioneered the practice of ordaining Holy Spirit–gifted women, demonstrating that women's ordination is blessed by God?

As someone who began ministry in a racially segregated Annual Conference, I thank God that Methodists elsewhere kept pushing for and eventually succeeded in forcing an end to the sin of the racist concoction of the Central Jurisdiction.

How would those denominations who have been wracked by clergy sexual abuse cover-up know the joys of collegial, episcopal oversight of clergy if United Methodists had not shown them how it's done? Let Methodists once again be the Research and Development arm of the Body of Christ, just like in Wesley's day.

Staying Together

As a bishop, my salary, authority, and position come from The United Methodist Church. Defending, advocating for, criticizing, and encouraging the UMC is my job. It's never my responsibility to help people disavow United Methodist ministry or to aid them in more comfortably, lucratively leaving our connection. I'm an officer of The United Methodist Church. If I find that I can no longer do that job, or if I conclude that the UMC is beyond redemption and reformation, I need to do the honorable thing and quit. Togetherness, keeping the Body of Christ in motion in mission is my vocation as a bishop, never disaffiliation or placidity won by infidelity to the dictates of our connection.

The only experience I've had with people separating from the church they vowed to "walk in the same all the days of your life" is as their pastor. Over the years, when people have threatened to leave my congregations, my responsibility is not only to ask why but also to ask, "Are you open to hearing reasons why I pray that you will not leave us?"

Clergy friends said, "What's the use of arguing? They've made up their minds. Besides, who are you to question them?"

I suspect that clergy don't plead with members who threaten to depart because their reasons may be painful to hear. That's sad because some separatists may be badly confused. Others may give candid feedback on our ministry that nobody else cares enough to give us.

When I've dared ask, here are some of the responses I've heard:

"You failed to call when my mother died."

"I'm tired of hearing politics from the pulpit."

"You should speak out more on important national issues."

"We have teenagers and this church's youth ministry is pitiful."

"We grew up Baptist and the worship at this church is not spiritual enough."

"Your preaching is too intellectual."

"You're not biblical enough in your sermons."

"You talk too much about the Bible."

"Unlike you, Joel Osteen's messages make me feel good about myself."

"I have yet to hear you preach a good sermon on hell."

Please note that most of these criticisms are focused on me, the pastor, showing how important expectations for the pastor are in most church members' minds and how we've misled people to believe that the pastor is the church.

Criticism of the pastor is an expected, predictable aspect of being a pastor. We live in a time of unprecedented criticism of leaders in church and out. Social media enables a few critics to have a large platform for their loud complaints. (Never have we had dozens of lawyers lined up on YouTube unabashedly pitching their services to help you split from the UMC. First consultation for free.)

Much of people's criticism of me is unjustified. ("Didn't even know that your dear mother had died. Sorry.") Some of it is related to problems with my personality that I can't change. ("You're not the first to tell me that I'm too impressed with myself. My mother would agree with you.") Some of the criticism is a commentary on the limits of my listeners and my lousy catechesis. When a man left my church because, "Not once have you voiced support for our President and his work to seal our borders from illegal Mexicans," I confessed, *Lord, forgive me for being a lousy teacher and preacher.*

And yet some critical comments are valuable criticism that few of my supporters in the congregation would dare to offer. ("Thank you. Could you say more? Can you help me to improve my work in this area?")

Buffeted by negative feedback? Congratulations on having a relationship, even with some of your unhappiest members, that gives them freedom to speak their minds.

Other critical comments by those on their way out regard congregational problems that also grieve you. ("Wow. I am also disappointed by our student ministry. How could we fix that?") If the disgruntled members threaten to leave, beg, "Please, please stay! I need your help to make this a more faithful church. Most of our members are clueless about our problems."

I haven't found any Methodists who are threatening to leave the UMC due to dissatisfaction with their pastor or congregation, making all the more sad that they are departing denominational United Methodism that (1) trained and sent them their pastor, (2) has little to do with the success or demise of their congregation, and (3) is irrelevant to their encounters with Christ in church or out.

Disaffiliation

Here's a portion of a document (*Disaffiliation from The United Methodist Church*) that was circulated among the congregation that produced me. It's fairly typical of what I've heard from those departing, indeed seems to be verbiage composed by some organization to aid those in need of a rationale for departure. (By the way: "Affiliation" is an inadequate description for what these self-described disaffiliates pledged when they joined the UMC. But I digress.)

The letter opens with an assertion of "irreconcilable theological differences" on "the authority of Scripture," "the importance of salvation vs. social activism," and "the size of the church bureaucracy, its significant cost, and its bureaucratic incompetency."

(The first two points are debatable on traditional, Wesleyan grounds. Wish more had been said. Check out the *BOD* where you'll find eloquent, faithful teaching on both scripture and salvation. Not sure what the third has to do either with theology or scripture. Dismantling bloated UMC bureaucracy is one thing on which all, right or left, agree.) Then, the self-described disaffiliates cite a "2019 UMC survey." When asked, "Which should be the primary focus of the UMC?" 68% of self-identified progressives picked, "Advocating for social justice to transform the world," and 70% of traditionalists opted for, "Saving souls for Jesus Christ." (Am I the only one who doesn't know what "progressive" and "traditionalist" mean when applied to Methodists?) Half of the "progressives" believed "there are ways to salvation that do not involve Jesus" while "86% of traditionalists believe the *only* way to salvation is through a relationship with Jesus." (Check that math.)

Every congregation I've served has had a diversity of beliefs on the meaning of "saving souls for Jesus Christ." Besides, if fellow Christians are wrong, don't you have an obligation to conversation that might lead to their correction rather than use this as an excuse for walking away? Talk, don't walk!

Then the document launches into a laundry list of aggrieved moments in UMC history like when "Chicago UMC Bishop Joseph Sprague denied the full deity and resurrection of Jesus Christ as well as the reliability of the Gospel John," Bishop Karen Oliveto warned not "to create an idol out of Jesus Christ," and someone named Thielen opposed "faith in a God of supernatural invention."

"Membership has steadily declined over the past half century, membership in Africa and Asia is growing" (true, but I doubt any Methodist in Africa has ever heard of Oliveto or Sprague).

Though the document denies that the desired division is "over one issue," the bulk of the grievances concerns arguments about, well, you guessed it, one issue:

American Methodists have been divided over the issue of homosexuality for fifty years. Every four years the issue is fiercely debated at the quadrennial Conference. Each time the progressives have lost. Currently the United Methodist church's *Book of Discipline* labels homosexuality a sin, bars the ordination of noncelibate homosexuals, and prohibits the blessing of same-sex marriages.... The *Book of Discipline* says that "the practice of homosexuality is incompatible with Christian teachings." The current *Book of Discipline* reflects Biblical teaching. The Bible says what it says. Several months ago, Don Cockrill went through a painstaking analysis of what the Bible says about homosexuality. Don concluded that the Bible is clear from the Old Testament to the New that practicing homosexuals are living in sin. Don concluded that to read the scriptures any other way is disingenuous...they don't care what the Bible says; they prefer the current progressives' embrace of that lifestyle as acceptable and conforming to the culture of the present world. Traditionalists say follow the scripture. While the *Book of Discipline*'s stance on homosexuality is traditional, it appears that a majority of General Conference delegates from the U.S. want to change it. The existing position is supported by a coalition of American traditionalists and delegates from overseas. So conservatives win the votes at General Conference every four years. But they have failed to take control of the denomination's seminaries or its bureaucratic structure who have reacted with defiance and organized resistance. The problem is that Methodist Bishops and various Conferences have refused to follow the *Book of Discipline* without consequences. The United Methodist Church does not have police to enforce compliance with the *Book of Discipline*. Self-avowed practicing homosexuals are being ordained for the ministry and same-sex marriages are being conducted. There is even a Queer Clergy Caucus.... In 2016 the church's Western Jurisdiction elected a gay San Francisco pastor, Karen Oliveto, as the first openly lesbian bishop in the United Methodist church.

United Methodism now has its first drag queen certified as an ordination candidate in Illinois. When performing as a drag queen, Isaac Simmons, dressed as a woman, uses the stage name Ms. Penny Cost (note the disrespectful play on words).... This same Northern Illinois Conference ordained transgender activist M. Barclay who self identifies as neither male nor female. I am fed up with the flouting of church disciplines by some bishops, some clergy and the UMC bureaucracy.

Glad this isn't about one issue. Don't know Don Cockrill, but any biblical scholar, including those who believe the Bible condemns same-sex relationships, knows that the Bible is anything but "clear" on the subject. If it were, we wouldn't be having this debate. Cockrill's interpretive confidence is, well, disingenuous.

A few biblical passages seem to condemn same-gender relationships as contrary to God's creation, but nobody knows what the Bible would say about adult, monogamous, faithful, long-term same-gender marriage. (Jesus doesn't show much interest in sexuality, gay or straight, marriage, or gender and says nothing about same-sex attraction.) But there is *no* biblical justification for making the issue paramount in one's "theological differences," no "scriptural authority" for making disagreements about gender orientation a sufficient rationale for "disaffiliation."

Next, the document invokes the 2020 "Protocol for Separation" that was concocted by a few bishops and caucus group leaders for the purpose of encouraging "the creation of a new conservative denomination that would retain traditional teachings...allows individual congregations by majority vote (50% + 1) to withdraw without forfeiting their property.... The new denomination would receive $25 M from the United Methodist Church." Sneaky "liberals changed their minds about the Protocol." The delay of General Conference 2022 is merely a "pretext" by church leaders who knew they would once again lose out to the "conservatives." Therefore, the only way "to have peace is to separate—shake hands, wish one another well, and go our separate ways."

I agree that it's tough for the church not to preach merely what's "acceptable and conforming to the culture of the present world." But who told the authors that same-sex sin (their one issue that's not the only issue) was the chief sin in the UMC, that the things they don't like among their fellow Christians are immune to Christ's transforming grace, or that the UMC is unredeemable? Not the Bible. Not Jesus (who makes not even a cameo appearance in most of these debates, maybe because there's no evidence that Our Lord gives a rip about the one issue that's not really their one issue).

It's inconceivable that some Methodists would mount these arguments in this way in any other cultural moment than the present when there's national political divisiveness among white folks who don't like the culture's racial reckoning and gender-issues debating. *Who's being culturally conforming now?*

Hey, disaffected, disaffiliating, you seem satisfied with the present state of your congregation (even though its median age is dangerously high; a fact unnoticed by your document). Is it possible that the things you like about your congregation are thanks to its association with the UMC? Are you sure that you should give Methodists halfway across the continent the power to force you out of the denomination that produced your congregation, all of your past pastors, the building that you didn't pay for but want to take with you, and sacramental encounters with Christ too numerous to mention? (Not to cut too close to the bone, but are you focused on Methodists on the west coast because that distracts you from the uncertain future of Methodism in your neighborhood?)

Am I being disingenuous? Guilty of worrying too much about Jesus and too little about the "authority of scripture"? Failing to get worked up over the one contemporary social issue that's not your main issue?

Sent into the Storm

Camping in a partially destroyed Methodist church with a hundred pastors of my Conference, working in the debris of Hurricane Katrina, for my evening devotional I chose Mark 6:45-51, Jesus and the storm at sea. I wanted to comfort clergy as they labored amid the devastation: Jesus comes to us on a storm-tossed sea, encourages and tells us not to fear.

> Jesus made his disciples get into a boat and go ahead to the other side of the lake.... After saying good-bye to them, Jesus went up onto a mountain to pray. Evening came and the boat was in the middle of the lake, but he was alone on the land. He saw his disciples struggling. They were trying to row forward, but the wind was blowing against them. Very early in the morning, he came to them, walking on the lake. He intended to pass by them. When they saw him walking on the lake, they thought he was a ghost and they screamed. Seeing him was terrifying to all of them. Just then he spoke to them, "Be encouraged! It's me. Don't be afraid." He got into the boat, and the wind settled down. His disciples were so baffled they were beside themselves. (Mark 6:45-51)

This time through the text, the discombobulating Holy Spirit showed me something I had never noted. A midnight sail on a potentially stormy sea was Jesus's idea. He didn't just suggest they risk it, "He made his disciples get into the boat and go ahead to the other side." They are in peril, in the middle of a storm-tossed sea in the dark of night because Jesus put them there.

Dare I contemplate that we're in a splintering, sputtering, baffling, fearful UMC because of Jesus?

Equally disconcerting is Mark's statement that "he came to them, walking on the lake. He intended to pass by them." What? *Pass by them?* Where was Jesus headed in his midnight stroll across the sea that was more important than coming to the aid and comfort of his disciples? Mark, do you mean to imply that Jesus has more important concerns than the care of his own followers? Is his mission larger than his twelve best friends who are huddled in his boat?

Still, Jesus detours from his larger purpose, speaks to his fearful, baffled followers in the boat, "Be encouraged! It's me. Don't be afraid."

Jesus not only comes to us, he climbs in the boat with us, and eventually the wind subsides. What faith Jesus has in us that he orders us—even with our fear and hopelessness—into the storm ahead of him. Though he has a larger mission than the church (the *navis*, a boat, is one of the earliest symbols for the church), he not only speaks to us, he climbs in the boat with us. Saved by him, we sail on, baffled by such love.

What New Creation?

Although the Global Methodist Church is not the only option for those wishing to "disaffiliate" from the UMC, it is the newest, a proposed denomination launched with a whimper rather than a bang. All I know of the GMC is what I've read in their public statements, their "Draft Discipline," and from conversations with those pastors and laity who, though flirting with the GMC, have been willing to talk with me.

From what I've learned about the GMC in its first months, here are some respectful questions I'd put to them:

- Do we really need yet another Protestant denomination? All indications are that denominationalism, as a way of organizing churches, has had its day. No new denomination addresses the decline that plagues Methodism; any new denomination must struggle with aging, graying, with children of various sexual orientations, abortions, racism, and a culture for whom church, any church, is optional. Listening to your spokespersons I wonder why you just don't go Free Methodist or Southern Baptist and forego all the rigmarole of starting a new denomination?

- How does the formation of a new denomination conclude the debate (on the single issue that's not the one issue) that you want to silence? I often hear, "I'm exhausted with the argument. I want to be in a church where some matters are settled once and for all." Trouble is, "traditional" and "progressive" are fluid categories. Who thinks that the labels "evangelical" or "liberal" mean anything anymore? Nobody, left, right, or center thinks the same way about LGBTQ+ issues that they thought just a decade ago. Things are liquid because the Holy Spirit likes it that way. Scripture refuses to speak definitively on some matters. UMC: Even after a split, there will be continuing tensions and debate. If dissension about same-sex inclusion could be silenced by a vote of General Conference, we would have. GMC: No prohibitive clergy rules or iron-fisted bishops will end all possibilities for tensions and debate. If Jesus had spoken more definitively on the one issue that preoccupies Methodists we wouldn't be in this mess. (Should we question our preoccupations?)

I know a lawyer who's made lots of money defending employers from claims by employees. He was full of enthusiasm for the GMC. Knowing how he made his living, I told him it was big of him to embrace the GMC's stand on collective bargaining.

"What?!" he exclaimed.

"I'm also surprised. Didn't seem to fit their rightwing politics. One of the few social justice issues that the GMC says that it's for is 'collective bargaining.' Not sure why that particular cause made it into their Draft Discipline while so many others were deleted, but there it is. Are you sure you want to leave the UMC for a church that promises rigidly to enforce—without negotiation or exceptions—the dictates of its Discipline?"

Speaking of lawyers, your Draft Discipline reads like it was written by one.

Long-term GMC comity has nothing to do with reaching "comity agreements" with the UMC. Denominational placidity will last until some GM makes a comment—possibly instigated by the Holy Spirit—and somebody else huffs, "You're a progressive in traditionalist clothing! How'd you get in here?" The name-calling, finger-pointing, and me-love-scripture-more-than-you bluster will resume, this time with folks you thought you had cleansed from your church.

• How will you evangelize new generations? The leadership of the GMC looks about as old as the UMC Council of Bishops. (I can't see that you've been able to recruit anybody to leadership who is not from one of the UMC conservative caucus groups. You look WCA all over.) The greatest challenge facing both denominations is limitation of the church to one generation—people over sixty.

Where's your "biblical authority" for that? The organization of and the issues that are driving the discussion within the GMC seem even more out of touch with Millennials than those of the UMC. You may have made a new denomination, but you seem even less concerned than the UMC about how to make young Methodists.

- I'm confused. You are unhappy with UMC bishops not having the backbone to be bishops who punish errant clergy. At the same time, you seem nervous about bishops flexing their muscle with congregations. Are you sure your rules resolve your issues with episcopal leadership? The plethora of prohibitive paragraphs in your Discipline suggest that the GMC is already anticipating fights over clergy and bishops. Methodist squabbling over internal, clergy concerns continues.

    I could show you how to make your Draft even shorter. All you've got to do is ask.

- What is your church for rather than against? GMC, do you really want to be known as, "The church that never…"? Pity the poor pastors who try to lead people who are attracted by your denomination's stand on one contemporary social issue (same-sex unions) that you swear is not your only issue. Many of you say that you are opposed to making "social justice" more important than "personal salvation." And yet here you are, trying to form a Wesleyan church on the basis of a position on one issue of social justice.

    Breakaway congregations tend to be unstable. Once people walk away from a church that disappoints them, they're likely to walk again, having misunderstood the nature of Christian congregating. Their search for the true, pure, right church that most comfortably aligns with their prejudices continues.

145

- By the way, in 1940, when the Southern Methodist Church left in protest against racial integration, like the GMC, they also boasted that they were leaving, not because of the one issue that everyone knew to be the issue, but rather due to their commitment to "scriptural holiness." Then there was the equally tiny Independent Methodist Church (1965) who also left because of holier-than-thou worries about Methodist racial mixing. Though you haven't heard of any of these diminutive denominations, their legacies of one-trick-pony politics ought to give you pause. You sure you will avoid their fate?

- Can you be certain that the UMC is a perversion of the Body of Christ? By leaving and forming a new church, you're not just saying that you don't like the way votes have gone at General Conference or that some bishops aren't the best leaders. You are saying that the UMC is unfaithful. Traditionally, Wesleyans have been reluctant to judge denominations from Assemblies of God to Roman Catholics. Are you sure there's no possibility of God doing a new thing (Isa 43:19) in the UMC? We've only been arguing over the one-issue-that's-not-the-one-issue for a mere forty years (Ps 90:4, 2 Pet 3:8). Give us more time.

   As a preacher, of course I know the frustration of being unable to talk others into my position on some important subject, even though I've backed up my sermons with scripture, a winning personality, and rhetorical flourish, all in twenty minutes. So I empathize with your anguish that, after years of dozens of sly articles in *Good News* and indignant WCA manifestos too numerous to mention, there are still some Methodists running loose muttering, "I see it differently." Sure, I've wished that Jesus would allow me to hammer, excommunicate, or at least arm wrestle my congregation into submission. Alas, Jesus doesn't work that way; yet, he never walked away from an argument or refused to be in conversation with even the most thick-headed of opponents.

That's why I'm baffled that your Draft Discipline doesn't explain why you are taking the drastic step of leaving one church to form another just because the church is full of people who are (as you see it) wrong.

Most of your Draft Discipline is filched from the UMC. (Why did you not lift "Our Theological Task" from the UMC *BOD*? It's some of the best parts of the book. It could help you be even more "orthodox.") That you have found so little in the UMC to reform gives credence to those who suspect that—in spite of your vehement denials—your denomination is being birthed in response to one contemporary social issue.

Ask anybody to take your Draft Discipline and compare it with the UMC *BOD*. Their question will be, "So what's your beef with the UMC?"

Here's the way some of my conversations have gone with GMC gurus. "We don't like…" *Neither do I.* "I'm tired of people not taking scripture seriously in regard to…" *Right on.* "He wouldn't know Chalcedonian Christology if it bit him in the behind." *Amen!* "The UMC *Book of Discipline* is a legalistic mess." *Like I've been saying for years.* "Therefore, we're leaving." *What?!*

• How come your Draft Discipline goes on and on about requirements for clergy candidates but says next to nothing about what clergy are for? What ought pastors be expected to produce? How will you judge if a pastor is incompetent? The UMC is paying dearly for our inability to state what sort of leadership it most needs from its clergy. Don't you want to fix that?

You're angry because some clergy weren't booted out of ministry so you've created the most powerful bishops in the history of Methodism who can kick out clergy faster than you can say, "To heck with due process." And you guys said you were leery of bishops!

You don't say how you will educate your candidates for ministry. (Could you already have in mind a seminary where you think it safe to send your candidates once it's emptied of UM seminarians?)

Strangest of all, Paragraph #405, 2 under "*Basic Qualifications* of the Ordained" (italics mine), "fidelity in Christian marriage between one man and one woman, chastity in singleness" comes before "knowledge and love of God" or "Have a call by God and the people of God." Really, GMC?

In eight years as a bishop, asking congregations, "What do you most need in a pastor to lead your congregation's mission?" never once did a congregation say, "marriage between one man and one woman." You've come a long way from Bishop Asbury's prohibition of married circuit riders, which is fine by me. But don't you think you're setting the clergy competence bar a bit low?

- You're asking clergy to cast their lot with a very small number of appointment possibilities, in one of the smallest Methodist bodies in the world, and with a polity that seems to value stability, seniority, and longevity over new leadership. No clergy from the big churches you are hoping to recruit are planning on going anywhere anytime soon. None are interested in being GMC without their large congregations. Little prospect for clergy mobility there.

You are also rallying around an issue (same-sex attraction and practice is contrary to God's will) that is of scant interest to younger cohorts. (Something like 80% of all Americans say the government ought not to prohibit same-sex marriage.) Your way of organizing church, while admirably simplified and downsized, is as boringly dated as the UMC. Have you learned nothing from UMC difficulties in calling a new generation of pastors?

Your Draft Discipline is a reaction against what you don't like about the present UMC rather than a catalyst for mission in a future beyond the UMC. You pay too high a compliment to the UMC *BOD,* giving great attention to solving the perceived problems of the UMC as a denomination but too little thought to a truly mission-driven reformation of Methodism. For example, rules about the election and limited tenure of bishops, as well as the ownership of congregational property, have been rewritten to reflect your unhappiness with the last couple of decades in the UMC. Looks like you think disagreement and dissention is a UMC problem that you are going to solve through new rules. Sorry, it's a continuing condition that you must muddle through. Disaffiliation is a passing storm; debates about human sexuality and social mores are a chronic condition like global warming.

In a decade or so, when asked by some young, upstart clergy, "Why are we doing church this way?" you'll have to say, "Well, you see, son, back in two thousand twenty something, there was a Methodist somewhere who was a drag queen and the best way we could express our outrage was by forming a new denomination that..." Get my drift?

Even if you manage to lure half a million Methodists to your new denomination in the next couple of years, that will be less than the Lord is taking into eternity.

- Considering that you continue the UMC *Book of Discipline*'s corporate America, legalistic style, can you be sure that just calling yourself "Global" purifies you of the nefarious legacy and practices of North American colonialism? Your way of being church is white-collar North American.

If you really aspire to be global, why not ask what is there about the UMC presentation of the gospel that enabled Africa to be such a bountiful area of vitality in the UMC?

• Got experience with independent congregations or clergy autonomy? Better ask some congregationalists for help making your modified call system work.

• You're angry that for the fourth or fifth time, you "won" the vote at General Conference to strengthen the prohibitions against same-sex unions and punish clergy who were neither married (defined as one man–one woman) nor celibate. No sooner was that won again by a small margin in St. Louis, than a large portion of the church said that General Conference couldn't force them into a position they thought was unwarranted by scripture. At their Annual Conferences the next year, "traditionalists" were cast off delegations, and replaced by "progressives." If we had a General Conference as planned, I'm sure the vote would be taken again and would be won by the progressives. General Conference voting doesn't solve this issue once and for all. It's a big distraction from our precipitous decline.

You're indignant that though the last vote went your way, a significant portion of the UMC doesn't feel bound by General Conference voting. I understand your disillusionment with the impotency of General Conference but can't figure out why you are creating a church that has so much faith in large, national, representative voting and episcopal enforcement. Roberts, of *Roberts Rules of Order*, wasn't a Methodist.

• How come your new Discipline looks so much like our old one? The best thing about your Draft Book of Discipline is its brevity. 125 pages. Way to go! (With just a bit more work, you could make it even shorter.) I envy the passion, downsizing the general church, ending bishops-for-life, abolition of jurisdictions, plans for paying bishops and DS's that are tied to what they actually do, the global emphasis, your affirmation that doctrine matters, and your upfront invocation of Christ (even though he isn't mentioned again once you begin churning out rules). Thanks for agreeing with me that the Judicial Council of the UMC is a mistake—though your "Connectional Council on Appeals" smells suspiciously like UMC litigiousness by another name. I liked your long section on ministry of the laity with its stress upon small groups though there's a lot of incipient individualism therein. Congregations owning their own buildings? Fine with me; maintaining costly real estate is draining the UMC. (But in an odd way, you're making building possession a mark of the church. You know as well as I there's no biblical authority for Christian real estate.) Glad to hear you invoke holiness but note that you fail to say what holiness means. (Remarriage after divorce? Covetousness? Gun violence? Domestic abuse? Addiction? Adultery? Environmental exploitation? Have you got a too-limited definition of "Holiness"?)

• I dislike the UMC apportionment system as much as you, but there's no way you can pay even for your downsized church with apportionments to congregations at the rate you propose. You're promising to remove congregations who don't pay their apportionments? Good luck with that.

• Love your Para 351—transfer of congregations to another Annual Conference. Our geographical Conferences are outdated and ossifying, another example of how we suppressed adaptive, supple service to mission.

Caucus Church

I don't envy that you're as much in the grip of politics of the right as some UMC leaders are to politics of the left. You are as beholden to caucuses and causes on the right (Good News, Wesleyan Covenant Association, Institute on Religion and Democracy) as the UMC to the left. The difference between the UMC and your GMC is that *you are exclusively the product of those caucuses.* You'll regret your thralldom to those who love their cause more than your congregations.

Wish you wouldn't attempt to love the Bible with talk of "Authority of Scripture" (not a traditionally Methodist category) and would talk more about the challenges of loving and obeying scripture's witness to a living, present Jesus Christ and his Holy Spirit expansive mission. Jesus doesn't come up that much in your defense of your new denomination. Is that a commentary on the limits of your theology or on the refusal of Jesus to be adapted for our usage of the moment?

I note that in Para 202, 3 you guys allow abortion if there's been "prayerful consideration" (!). Good old American individualism, freedom of choice, rendering abortion personal and private. The muddled paragraphs on abortion in the UMC *BOD* couldn't have said it any less theologically.

Para 306 says the GMC is "called to inclusiveness," a surprising use of a secular, nonbiblical term. Ditto "openness, acceptance, and support." Ditto "Global." (Come on, can't you find a more biblical, christological name for your church than "Global"?)

You claim that your denomination will control rather than be controlled by cultural forces. A noble goal. However, a new denomination, birthed by a debate within North American culture, won't get you there. Nor can compliant clergy be convened and governed simply by better enforcement of rules. The only good reason for your leaving the UMC is disagreement about Christ and nothing you've said about Christ differs from anything the UMC taught you about Christ.

You pay lip service to mission in the GMC Draft Discipline, but you're organizing yourself in much the same way as the UMC, allowing internal denominational order, discipline, clergy concerns, statements about social issues, and self-serving congregational prerogatives to take precedence over coordinating for mission.

An official of a Free Methodist Seminary (kept afloat by funding and students from the UMC), gushes enthusiasm at the launch of the "next Methodism" "out of the ashes of the current tragedy known as the United Methodist Church" (https:// timothytennent.com/next-methodism/). Even though the man's academic background is exclusively within non-Methodist seminaries, he charges that UM seminaries and bishops caused us to lose "our identity as a distinctive Christian movement." That's a bit harsh, don't you think?

While he admits that "the GMC cannot be built on the foundation of what we are 'against,'" his own caucus-scripted polemic shows how tough that will be. As with all GMC apologists, he purports to lament, "One of the false narratives...which has gained significant traction is that the split in United Methodism is over the ordination of men and women who are in same-sex marriages." His most recent book? You guessed it. Over two hundred pages on the peril of same-sex love.

Typical of GMC operatives, the good doctor makes the required, though absurd, claim that disaffected Methodists are actually not leaving; poor things have been "swept out the door into the streets." Talk about "false narrative." Not one single instance of anyone being kicked out of a UMC church for GMC sympathies. Perpetrator playing the victim.

Anyway, this presumptive leader of the GMC urges his new denomination (that he says proudly joins the ranks of "*40,000 denominations* in the world," italics mine) to plant churches or else go down with "a decaying civilization." A January 2022 gathering of "fine Methodist theologians"—retrieved from the flotsam and jetsam of the "current tragedy known as the United Methodist Church"—has got his back.

Like I say, you've got your work cut out for you, dear disaffiliating doctor. In interviews with dozens of pastors on their way out of the UMC, not one voiced a desire to plant new churches. Maybe your seminary can fix that, though without UMC scholarships and students.

I know, I know. The GMC hopes to silence pushback like mine by bolting the "the current tragedy known as the United Methodist Church." Still, if my respectful questions give some fellow UMs the courage to continue to collaborate with the innovative Holy Spirit in the hope of a new UMC, I'm glad I spoke up.

Chapter 9

HOPEFUL
TOGETHER

My experience with separation is limited to my work as pastor to the marriages in my congregations. I began this book by comparing what's happening in the UMC to the grief work of a funeral. A better metaphor may be the breakup of a marriage.

Attempting to console a woman whose husband had bolted for another with whom he was more comfortable, I said, "You are going through grief at the loss of your marriage."

She responded, "Grief? Grief doesn't do justice to the half of it. If he were dead, I wouldn't have a problem. He's alive, headed toward a new life with a sizeable share of our property, taking with him the life that we had. I'm not in grief, I'm angry!"

Togetherness is what Jesus does; separation is our rejection of what Jesus wants. We're not at a dignified funeral for the UMC; we're entering a lawyer-on-lawyer custody fight in family court.

When I would hear that a couple in my church was thinking of divorce, I always reached out. "Can we talk?" (Thus my claim that whenever separation threatens, it's a time for talk, talk, talk.)

Conversation with people in pain, those who feel victimized, or who are angry with one another is risky. But as pastor, it's my job. Though I tried to be a good listener, I felt compelled fairly early to say, "Let me be honest. As a pastor, I'm prejudiced toward togetherness. You promised to stay together so I'll probably push you to do just that.

"Can't force you to stay married. Got no quick fixes, but (unless this is a situation of adultery, spouse abuse, or domestic violence) my job is to press you to do the forgiveness, truth-telling, and hard work required to stay together. Togetherness—in church, marriage, family, friendship, or church—in spite of acrimonious arguments, is better than separation. I've got Jesus backing me up. Scripture too. Now, let's talk."

It was up to the couple whether or not to continue, but I felt the church had to be true to our promise, made at their wedding, to support them in keeping their promises.

I pulled out arguments on behalf of togetherness: Did you know that research shows there are predictable seasons of marital unhappiness, having less to do with the condition of the marriage than with different stages of adulthood? Are there just two things each of you could do that might enable you to stay together? Do you need to make more time during the week to communicate? Can you be more regular in your church attendance? Would Jesus command you to forgive? Is there an unproductive argument—that neither of you has any chance of winning—that needs to be put on ice?

Then I laid on them the old, "In your marriage vows, God has promised that, if you keep your vows to stay together, God would bless your fidelity. So, God didn't keep God's promises?"

Friendly Divorce?

"We're going to have a friendly divorce," some couples would say. While I applauded their intentions, truth forced me to say that their desire for an amicable separation was probably a delusion. When love and promises are broken, expect pain, resentment, anger. Separation is not only, "I don't want to live with you anymore," it's also "Who'll get the children? Who will live in the house?" That's why most divorcing persons end up despising lawyers. Lawyers not only profit handsomely from divorce but also (and it pains me as a pastor to admit this) attorneys are often the sole realistic truth-tellers. "You want a divorce? It will cost you. Who gets the house? Who gets Christmas?"

(I hope all you online lawyers who are rushing in to make money off a Methodist divorce are honest with your clients about the non-monetary costs of separation.)

Advocates of the ill-fated "Protocol" vainly hoped that through this "comity agreement" the UMC could avoid years of costly lawyers' fees. A fantasy equivalent to the "friendly divorce."

A frequent source of sadness was my suspicion that the couple was attempting to solve, through separation, problems that had little to do with their marriage: "I'm miserable being fifty [or having a dead-end job, or being addicted, or being depressed] and can't do anything about that, so I'll do something about you. I'm leaving. Er, uh, I mean 'disaffiliating.'"

Lord, give me a way to say, "Your best means of coming out on the other side of your personal unhappiness is having someone who has vowed to be with you through your sadness. Stay together! Work it out! Continue the argument!"

In our present church fragmentation, I suspect that some of us are saying, "I can't change the current culture so I'll change my church, hoping that will give me more control of my environment."

Pastors learn to be suspicious about the reasons couples give for separating. When people complain, "The United Methodist Church is too liberal," maybe they're saying that they're feeling out of control. "I don't like our progressive bishop," may mean, "I don't want to lose the church I have loved."

They may also be saying, "My church is advocating discipleship that is not the comfortable, less engaged, less accountable affiliation that I thought I was buying when I joined the UMC."

(GMC, you make a big deal out of marriage as one man/one woman, making it a major attribute of your clergy. How come you don't condemn the dissolution of marriage? Jesus sure did. Some of your denominational leadership have had difficulty staying married, probably about the same proportion as UM leadership, but still. Thought you were big on the "authority of scripture.")

When a church member says, "I'm leaving this congregation because you are unbiblical, unfaithful, and liberal," if I mount no defense, separatists are justified in believing that the web accusation of a caucus group is true.

Some of our division is a commentary on the way we have allowed current political allegiances and media silos to overcome our vocation to be salt and light to the world. (If I can't shout you into silence, I'll lock myself into that gated community of buddies who think as I.) There's confusion between the Kingdom of God and the USA, an inability to tell the difference between a thinking, caring American and a called, witnessing Christian. When "progressive" or "traditionalist" become more determinative than "Methodist," it's a sign that simplistic North American political polarities have overcome biblically authorized identity.

Those who say, "Let 'em go. We'll be a better church after they leave," are kidding themselves. The UMC will be weaker after a split: loss of financial resources along with some of our dearest, most vital congregations, and a few of our most creative, entrepreneurial pastors. Progressives will also lose some of their most adept, doggedly persistent, Bible-loving interlocutors, leaving you stuck in a denominational echo chamber with an even higher percentage of people who think just like you.

In my years of interaction with those whose unhappiness is now boiling over into a desire to depart, er, uh, I mean *disaffiliate*, I've learned much from my conversations with dissidents. So I beg of you, please don't abandon me to my theological blind spots! Though you are wrong in your belief that you love scripture more than I, some of your pompous, painful, hard-to-hear criticism of my theological views is, worst of all, *true*!

Loving an Imperfect Union

Amid my lament of our current splintering, I recall that most growth over last fifty years in congregations has been accomplished through diversity and variety of worship options, hymnody, small groups, and programs. Congregations who were initially reluctant to move to multiple worship services for fear that they would foster fragmentation found that their diverse offerings increased attendance. As we've noted, the UMC is the product of separations and mergers. The university where I work has served four different Methodist denominations. Every formerly large UMC congregation in my town is dwindling, not because it's too diverse, but because the world can't tell one beige, bland, leftward-leaning, generically Methodist congregation from another.

Maybe Jesus is saying to me, as he said to his disciples who complained that there were some who wanted to work with him but not with them, "Enough of your infighting. Lighten up. Whoever isn't adamantly against us is probably for us" (Mark 9:40), or words to that effect.

If your congregation wants to live up to its membership promises, then I urge adamancy in finding a beguiling, compelling way to testify: *We're not leaving! God's got a good thing going here and we're not damaging it by allowing ourselves to be drawn into denominational squabbling. Got a gripe with the way our congregation worships and serves Jesus Christ? We're all ears. A beef with bishops or General Conference? Big deal. Stay focused!*

In discussions, be honest and charitable about the perfectly good reasons that might tempt someone to leave the UMC but also tell the truth about all the good reasons for staying. Urge, beg people not to leave the argument. Listen, but also be willing to debate if someone libels Methodist saints by unjustly accusing them of biblical, doctrinal, or evangelical infidelity.

I know a Conference where a dozen of the most talented, proven, youngish clergy have left the pastoral ministry—without even a "sorry to see you go." Pastors, let such episcopal passivity encourage you to be courageous and speak up, argue, and plead, "Please, stay in the conversation! We need you!" While I may not be smart or persuasive enough to talk you out of leaving, I can express my grief at your going.

Fight to keep your congregation in the UMC, urging people not to walk that perilous path of being a virtually independent congregation in a very small, aging, mostly white denomination whose future is even less assured than the large, aging, mostly white UMC.

UMC bishops: Preserving the church that called and consecrated you is your fiduciary responsibility. Don't waste time helping dismantle the church you are consecrated to protect, preserve, and perpetuate. Defend the faith in the UMC as a body uniquely blessed by Christ. Protect loyal, promise-keeping United Methodists who don't want to be pushed out of their church by a group of determined, though confused and disloyal, Methodists.

The Council of Bishops is a warning: keep quiet, smiling, affirming, uncritically listening, attempting to cut a deal with lawyered up bullies who threaten litigation, make division worse. You'll empower those who have long been loudly adamant about leaving while demoralizing steadfast members who quietly want to stay UMC.

Leaders, lay and clergy, must find ways boldly to say to their congregations, "Let me assure you, when you joined the UMC, we told you the truth. You are in a church that is scripturally sound, fully attentive to the demands of Jesus Christ, and doing all it can to engage you in Christ's mission. You must not believe the relatively small number of the disaffected who are impugning the fidelity of the UMC and its members."

It's good to listen to why people are taking the drastic step of leaving. Perhaps you'll be better for what you hear. Rather than sitting back passively and letting people vote, be active participants in the debate. When bishops speak of a "gracious exit" and of showing "respect" to all participants, even to those who pass judgment upon the church these bishops are pledged to defend, the bishops' graciousness is self-protection from learning how to lead painful, difficult, contentious conversations. As every pastor knows, it takes courage to hold people accountable, not only to listen but also to attempt to teach, to tell the truth, and, if God wills, to correct and to convert them.

Beginning in the 1960s and throughout the 1970s, the UMC saw the rise of caucuses, Methodists who gathered around shared, hyphenated, causal identity. Caucusing Methodists moved from concern, to conviction, to a cause, to an organized caucus, and usually to a campaign. Perhaps the oldest of these caucuses is Good News, fertile parent of the Confessing Movement, the Mission Society for United Methodists, Aldersgate Renewal Ministries, the Foundation for Theological Education, Lifewatch, RENEW, Transforming Congregations, the Association for Church Renewal, and United Methodist Action (the Methodist wing of the Institute of Religion and Democracy, or IRD.)

Close to thirty caucuses both fragmented United Methodism (or perhaps highlighted fragmentation that was already there) and encouraged inward preoccupation with the denomination. There were caucuses *for* Hispanics, gays, lesbians, various Asian peoples, Native Americans, and ordination of women, and there were caucuses *against* abortion, empowering of homosexuals, constraints on missions, and ordination of women.

Church by caucus could be seen as one of the most positive aspects of the old UMC when we lived up to Wesley's words, "In essentials, unity; in non-essentials, liberty; in all things, charity."

Through caucusing, Methodists recognized, permitted, and even affirmed differences within our church in order to keep the maximum number of Methodists arguing under our big tent. The caucuses took credit for the election and direction of bishops, kept hot-button issues in front of us (whether we wanted to hear about them or not), and made the UMC a wonderfully unwieldly, life-giving, intellectually interesting, spiritually expansive place to be—together.

Yet when some of the more conservative (they prefer "orthodox") caucuses began openly and unashamedly to talk separation and divorce, they crossed a line. Their move toward schism was predictable after decades of obsession with internal clergy concerns and carping complaint against their fellow

Methodists. Still, when a caucus like the Confessing Movement moved from constructive criticism to destructive schism, they violated one of the purposes of the church: forbearing one another in love.

Hey, WCA, check out the data on studies of the unhappiness of people after their divorce (higher than the unhappiness of married couples who stay and fight). May make you think twice before you "disaffiliate."

If one is unhappy with the UMC, resist, advocate, protest, but once you threaten to leave you kill the conversation. For most of my ministry, *Good News* magazine has been an often helpful, sometimes uncomfortable partner. But now that *Good News* is walking (stomping?) away, the UMC has lost a once valuable witness. In its most recent issue (July/August 2022), *Good News* excoriated for "misinformed" beliefs, breaking "the bonds of trust we had created," "Because they lost." Loyal UMs were called "angry institutionalists" who were being led by "Leaders who have proven themselves duplicitous and hypocritical" by "demanding their piece of flesh." *Good News* charged that "our hopes for a mutual 'bless and send' approach to separation ... is being replaced by 'tear and rend.'" UMC is only "twisting rules and trust clauses to maintain dying institutions."

On the day when *Good News* removes "Leading United Methodists…" from their front cover and admits to its true identity as propagandist for the GMC, it forsakes its proud history of nasty, sometimes perceptive and helpful criticism of the UMC that nobody else had the courage to say. We'll be poorer for it.

As a pastor, when counseling a couple in marital distress, I knew that if either member of the couple dared to speak even of the possibility of divorce, they probably would divorce.

Something like the GMC was inevitable when *Good News* moved from being a magazine that urged more biblical accountability to threatening that they would walk away if the conversation didn't go their way. For more than a decade, "good" in *Good News* has meant good-bye.

One of the *Discipline*'s few reasons for removing a pastor is for a pastor surreptitiously to start a new congregation in another denomination. Yet some bishops are allowing clergy to do just that. One dissident tells me he's exiting because his bishop didn't kick out a woman who performed a same-sex marriage, failing to note that the same bishop has allowed this man to receive full salary and benefits, even as he preaches schism, badgering his congregation to leave the UMC. Ironic, huh?

Throughout church history, nobody has ever admitted to being a schismatic. Still, Dante put schismatics all the way down next to Satan in the eighth circle of *The Inferno* (below heretics at circle six, way below the lustful and gluttonous). While Dante wasn't a Methodist, still, think twice before you take that big step.

Talented graduating seminarians are being turned away by Conferences with "we have no room for you" while pastors are appointed to pulpits where they are openly preaching schism. Confrontation, discipline, and accountability of pastors (what bishops vow to oversee in the bishops' consecration) take courage. Whence comes courage? From commitment to the mission of Jesus Christ.

GMC, do you really want to be led by someone who was a bishop in the UMC, paid entirely by funds from the UMC, who, while being paid by the UMC, worked surreptitiously to dismantle the UMC?

Even Amid the Storm, Hope

The UMC ought to take a good look at the proposed GMC and see what we can incorporate of their insights. I wish the UMC called our *BOD* the "Transitional Book of Discipline" just like the GMC. God didn't create our church structures and rules; we can transition them out in order to keep up with God.

The UMC cannot be preserved as we have known it. Let's seize our coming financial, organizational crisis as opportunity to do the urgent creative dismantling and simplification that we should have summoned the courage to do long ago.

Why duplicate ministries? Let the conversation begin on how the UMC and GMC can cooperate. Mission? Camps? Institutions for the aging? Military chaplains? UMCOR? UMVIM? Seminaries? (GMC, would you like to have half of the thirteen UM seminaries we can no longer support?) Not sure how far these discussions would go because the GMC is detaching itself from the thousands of unproductive, unsustainable, denominationally dependent UMC congregations as well as from our colleges, and facilities for children and the aging that have long been a financial burden for the UMC but whose work we think is essential for Christian witness.

Is the GMC really willing to receive a congregation that has voted by only two-thirds or a simple majority, or three-fourths or whatever, to leave the denomination, meaning that those who voted against leaving will be taken unwillingly into a different church from the one they joined? Wouldn't want to be a pastor of that.

Some of you know what it's like to be a minority who pushes back against the majority. My fear is that—after enduring our sad, acrimonious divorce and after being forced out of the UMC by a vote of their fellow Methodists—many will leave church altogether, joining the burgeoning ranks of the "Dones."

"Methodism? Been there, done that."

We must continually be willing to account for the hope that is within us (1 Pet 3:15). My hope is not for some knock-down argument for staying UMC. Those who have been devising strategies for separation for decades and have at last come out of the closet and have been empowered and legitimized by the errant "Protocol," will not easily be convinced to forego divorce and stay UMC. But then, no church has been constituted by or survived through arguments, by being on the same page in our believing, or by having reached a middle-of-the-road compromise. We are saved by Christ who loves to reconcile.

Who knows what's ahead for either the GMC or the UMC? Turning around any church whose median age is so high is daunting. The existence of the church has been contested since the first congregation of Christians, and no church has lived except through adaptation, reformation, and reorganization, some provoked by external pressures, some due to internal critics, all under the possible instigation of or resistance to the Holy Spirit.

What is certain is that the church of Jesus Christ—God's answer to what's wrong with the world, the peculiar way Christ has chosen to take up room in order to save us—is not defeated. If it is cast down by our ineptitude and infidelity, Christ shall raise up a new generation of Christians more faithful than we. If the church dawdles, dwindles, and dies in one part of town, it shall be resurrected elsewhere. Should our great cathedrals crumble, Jesus will insinuate himself into some shabby storefront ministry without missing a beat. If a church's leaders are boring and cowardly in our oversight of God's people, God shall shove forward others to assume the mantle of leadership. If a church shortcuts being the Body of Christ by devising and enforcing rules, attempting by majority vote to silence the witness of a vocal minority, punishing the most creative, and rewarding the bean counters and rule-keepers, the Holy Spirit is capable of shaking the foundations, firing the lawyers, breaking our regulations, dethroning our idols, setting fire to our stuff, and giving voice to the voiceless (Acts 2). Gospel triumphs over law. If God forsakes, defunds, and refuses to bless one ministry, God miraculously initiates another. If a church becomes the lapdog of the powerful and comfortable, time and again God has shown a willingness to cast down the privileged and preach good news to the poor. If a church cowers in the safe, uncontested middle, God struts even more recklessly among the marginalized. If a church fails to welcome those whom Jesus drags in the door, they and Jesus will take a hike, so determined is Christ not to allow the church to determine the boundaries of his kingdom. Nothing is more certain in this life than the victory of Christ, bringing along with him into glory his rag-tag congregation of improbable, unreconciled but being reconciled, squabbling saints, his dear but beleaguered Bride, his besmirched but beloved church.

There is little reason to believe that the GMC is forming a denomination appreciably better than the UMC it seeks to supplant. *And* the UMC cannot survive in the form we have known it; indeed, why should it? That's the Holy Spirit for you, disrupting, renewing everything it touches, God refusing to let us be, God in motion toward us, ready or not, God taking us along for the ride. Resurrection.

Our future with God is conditioned by neither the UMC nor the GMC. Therefore, we have hope. In the Holy Spirit, God goes local, empowering all for participation in Christ's mission to bring all things together under his lordship. That's why we grieve not for the UMC or the GMC as those who are hopeless.

Because Jesus Christ loves to raise the dead and to transform anybody he meets, amid the turbulence of our separations, fragmentations, and accusations, we can rest easy in the faith that these words are trustworthy and true, "I know the plans I have in mind for you, declares the LORD; they are plans for peace, not disaster, to give you a future filled with hope" (Jer 29:11). Hope.

John ends his Gospel by taking us to the beach after a horribly catastrophic, death-dealing storm otherwise known as the crucifixion of the Son of God (John 21:1-21). A gaggle of disciples have gone back to what they know best. Fishing. But though they fish all night, they have nothing to show for it.

Early in the morning, just at dawn, a stranger appears on the beach calling to them:

> "Children, have you caught anything to eat?" They answered him, "No." He said, "Cast your net on the right side of the boat and you will find some." So they did, and there were so many fish that they couldn't haul in the net. Then the disciple whom Jesus loved said to Peter, "It's the Lord!" When Simon Peter heard it was the Lord, he wrapped his coat around himself (for he was naked) and jumped into the water. The other disciples followed in the boat, dragging the net full of fish....

The stranger fed them with bread and some of the (to be exact) 153 fish they had miraculously hauled in. After breakfasting on the beach, Jesus asked Simon Peter three times the same question: "Do you love me?" A short time before, Simon had thrice denied even knowing Jesus. Now, three times Simon declares his love for Jesus.

Jesus tells Simon to "Feed my lambs" and "Take care of my sheep." Then, after predicting the manner that Peter would pay dearly for loving such a savior, Christ commands, "Follow me."

Methodists, here's our parable. Maybe the disciples wanted to look back and dwell on their failures faithfully to follow Jesus in the past, their disputes with one another, or their multiple misunderstandings of Jesus. Never the brightest candles in the box, their corporate cowardice at the foot of the cross is undeniable.

"Enough of this Jesus movement, let's go back to where we're most comfortable—fishing."

But that's not good enough for the risen Christ. He comes back to them (once again they don't seek him; he sought them), appearing to them in the darkness, just before dawn. Even though they have been with Jesus every step of the way, they don't recognize him. "Who are you?" (John 21:12).

Sometimes those closest to Jesus, those working for him, are the least likely to see him when he shows up, unable to recognize him moving among them in the darkness just before dawn.

There's a sermon begging to be preached, had I the time and you the patience.

Jesus asks Peter repeatedly "Do you love me?" giving Peter three opportunities to affirm his faith. Peter steps up to the challenge. The risen Christ doesn't look back and recount all the instances when Peter behaved as if he didn't love him; rather Jesus calls Peter forward into a new day, offering him a chance to get mission right, helping Peter to focus on what's most important, giving him specific work to do in his name. (Not the past tense, "Peter, did you love me?" but the present and future, "Do you love me?") Christ moves Peter from mere declarations of love to a command for loving activity in this world, right now, into the future.

Christ's parting words are vocational, missional: "Follow me."

Fellow Methodists, the risen Christ is talking to us. He wants us to succeed. Don't look back; look forward. As Jesus admonished, "Remember Lot's wife" (Luke 17:32) who looked back and was turned into a pillar of salt (Gen 19:26), which seems a rather severe punishment for nostalgia. Still, you've been warned.

Focus on what's important. Center your attention on Him who put you into Methodist Christianity in the first place. Look to Jesus. Listen to and obey Jesus. To us, amid any of our losses, differences, grief, anger, and all the rest, he keeps asking, "Do you love me?"

When it comes down to it, wherever in the Body of Christ you find yourself, with whatever tasks are set before you, that's the question, Christ's only question, "Do you love me?"

And then the call, his summons, how we got to be Methodists in the first place, our mission, our hope, love in action, all Jesus ever wanted, don't look back, "Follow me."

Will Willimon can't remember when he was not a Methodist. Yet he hopes never to forget his ordination promise to "share in the ministry of Christ and of the whole church: by preaching and teaching the Word of God." His memoir, *Accidental Preacher*, tells how Christ commandeered his life through The United Methodist Church. Serving as a Methodist pastor, campus minister, seminary professor, and bishop, Will has taught at Duke Divinity School for four decades and has preached in, advised, and consulted with hundreds of congregations. His ninety books have sold over a million copies. Among his Abingdon books on being Methodist are *Rekindling the Flame: Strategies for United Methodism* (with Robert L. Wilson); *A New Connection: Reforming the UMC* (with Andy Langford); *This We Believe: The Core of Wesleyan Faith and Practice*; *Why I Am a United Methodist*; and now, *Don't Look Back*.

Other Abingdon Press Books by Will Willimon

God Turned toward Us
Listeners Dare
Preachers Dare
Stories by Willimon
Fear of the Other
Who Lynched Willie Earle?
Pastor, Revised Edition
Resident Aliens (with Stanley Hauerwas)

Additional Resources for *Don't Look Back*

Visit abingdonpress.com/dontlookback to find resources for pastors and congregations, including a Leadership Resource Guide and Video Series. The **Leadership Resource Guide** (PDF) includes:

1. The outline for a four-part sermon series
2. A simple plan for leading the church's leadership team in a guided reading & discussion process over a two-month period, including
   - readings from the book and questions for reflection
   - suggestions for discussing and processing
   - questions to facilitate wise decision-making
   - prompts to help leaders determine the church's next steps
3. A simple plan for a one-day church retreat for ministry leaders and volunteers
   - helps the pastor to facilitate a process where church folks address together the six challenges (chapter 6) and the leadership team's proposed next steps
   - provides a series of clarifying questions to guide the retreat

The **Video Series** includes three brief videos where Will Willimon addresses congregations directly with words of challenge, encouragement, and inspiration. The videos may be used as part of the sermon series, the leadership team discussion, or the church retreat.

These resources are designed to help congregations move forward with a clear view of what's next for their church and a realistic plan for achieving it. Congregations that go through this process will create a future full of hope!

Printed in the USA
CPSIA information can be obtained
at www.ICGtesting.com
LVHW030742121023
760407LV00005B/15